WALTER OF BIBBESWORTH

THE TREATISE
Le Tretiz
of

WALTER OF
BIBBESWORTH

Translated from the Anglo-Norman by

ANDREW DALBY

*with the Anglo-Norman text as established by William Rothwell
and published by the Anglo-Norman Online Hub*

PROSPECT BOOKS
2012

First published in 2012 by Prospect Books,
Allaleigh House, Blackawton, Totnes, Devon TQ9 7DL.

© 2012, English translation and editorial matter, Andrew Dalby.
© 2009, Anglo-Norman text, William Rothwell.

The English text and editorial matter was first printed by Prospect Books in the journal *Petits Propos Culinaires* 93 (2011).

BRITISH LIBRARY CATALOGUING IN PUBLICATION DATA:
A catalogue entry of this book is available from the British Library.

Typeset by Lemuel Dix.
The cover illustration is a detail from a stained-glass window depicting scenes from the life of St Mary the Egyptian, in the cathedral at Bourges (13th century). Image courtesy of the Bridgeman Art Library.

ISBN 978-1-903018-86-6

Printed and bound by the Gutenberg Press, Malta.

CONTENTS

      þe childe   *born*
E quant li emfez serra neez

      swaþclut
Coveint k'il seit maylolez,

    cradel
Puis en berce le cochez

      a rockere
8   E de une bercere vous purveez.

            to crepe
Le enfant comence a chatener

Einz k'il sache a peez aler.

     slaverez
E quant il baave de nature,

          fro slavering
12   Pur ces dras sauver de baavure

         to his rockere
Dites dounc a sa bercere

         a slavering clout
Ke ele lui face une baavere.

E quant comence de aler

     cley   *bilagge him*
16   De tay se veet espaluer,

    laminge   *hurting*
E pur maine e pur blesure

Garszoun ou garce li deit suire,

    stomble   *falle*
Qu'il ne cece ne ne chece.

Lines 5–19 of Le Tretiz *of* Walter of Bibbesworth *(manuscript G), showing how the English glosses are interlineated with the Anglo-Norman text. In the original text that we have printed parallel with the modern English translation, we have omitted these glosses in the interests of clarity. Of course, the full version may be seen in the Anglo-Norman Hub edition on line (see references below), and almost all the glosses are referred to or discussed in the footnotes to the modern translation.*

PREFACE

This *Treatise*, written nearly eight centuries ago to help an English mother to teach two young children French, triumphantly surpasses its purpose. Used for the next two hundred years by many others, young and old, as a language textbook, then temporarily forgotten, it has been reborn as a source of information for scholars of Anglo-Norman, Old French, Middle English, and the material history of medieval England. It deserves to be better known still.

Walter of Bibbesworth's book is among the very earliest, in any language, intended for children to hear and read. Walter knew his audience. Skilfully, humorously, he keeps his readers amused as he surveys the English and French lexica of childhood, housework, farm work, fishing, baking, brewing and entertaining; as he lists animal cries and collective nouns; as he lets his rhymes run away with him, teases us with an occasional riddle, and whets our appetite with his High Feast.

The *Treatise* is interesting not only for itself but also for its social and personal context. The language politics of England in Walter's time – the privileged position of French and the ascendancy of those who spoke it – was about to change. The *Treatise* itself was, in a way, the first sign of this change. Bilingualism would not survive naturally; French needed to be taught. Walter wrote his book (as a wedding present, probably) for his neighbour and friend Dionisie de Anesty. They could not have guessed this when the gift was made, but Dionisie's stepdaughter, the little girl who was to learn French with Walter's help, was to marry into the greatest family in the kingdom.

I hope I have done justice to Walter's book, and that this translation will bring him even more readers. I hope, in the footnotes, that I have clarified Walter's train of thought (not too difficult) and shown how his work relates to the speech of England in his time. My thanks to William Rothwell and the Anglo-Norman Text Society for allowing us to provide a text of Walter's original French face to face with the English translation. This plain text is borrowed from Rothwell's new, annotated on-line edition at www.anglo-norman.net/texts/bibb-gt.pdf.

My thanks, too, to Tom Jaine of Prospect Books for proposing this most enjoyable project; to Rothwell again, and William Sayers, and the other scholars whose work on the *Treatise* guided my path; to the London Library for books and more, and to friends at the Oxford Food Symposium. And, most of all, to Maureen.

Andrew Dalby
Saint-Coutant, 2 March 2012

INTRODUCTION

The story of this *Treatise* begins with the story of the people who made it. We are in the early 1230s; we are somewhere in Hertfordshire; and there's a man and a woman involved.

We don't know, and probably we will never know, how Walter de Bibbesworth and Dionisie de Anesty met. We know (as well as medieval personal facts are ever known) that they were both from minor landed families, living about fifteen miles apart. Walter was from Bibbesworth Hall near Kimpton; his family also owned manors in Essex. Dionisie was the only child of Nicholas de Anesty who lived in Anstey Castle and farmed the land around it. We may observe that at Hertford, roughly half way between them, there had been twice-weekly markets ever since the year 905; a bigger draw for those who farmed on a large scale was the new, week-long Hertford Fair, granted by King Henry III in 1226 and held on the last week in October. Wherever they met, their contacts went beyond polite formality, but we don't know how far beyond. Walter was something of a soldier, and he thought of himself as a poet, a troubadour even. Dionisie had been married and widowed; then, still young, she caught the eye of a middle-aged gentleman of much greater wealth and influence than herself or Walter.

This gentleman was Warin de Munchensi (*de Monte Canisio* in Latin documents: no one knew where Mount Canisius was). As the eventual result of a succession of family alliances, he had inherited a swathe of property across southern England, from Kent to Herefordshire.[1] So appetizing were the de Munchensi possessions that although Warin, like his ancestors, had never done anything in war or politics he had still come to mind as a suitable candidate when the Earl of Pembroke,

---

1.   He is described as lord of Swanscombe in Kent, and so he was; also as lord of Painswick in Gloucestershire, and so he was; others emphasize his holdings in Essex. There is, I think, no source to tell us where he most often lived.

hereditary Marshal of England, sought a husband for his sister Joan. In 1220 or thereabouts Joan had married Warin. Then, in 1234, Joan had died, leaving him with two small children.

When Warin de Munchensi proposed to fill the vacancy by marrying Dionisie, it may well be imagined that her father Nicholas saw no reason to hesitate. They married and she immediately found herself in charge of an large household and two children who were likely to rise higher in the kingdom than their father ever had.

This needs explaining. Joan, Warin's first wife, had been slow to marry, slow to produce children and early to die, but her family background was impeccable. She was one of the five daughters, one of the ten children, of the famous William Marshal, the greatest warrior of the early thirteenth century, King John's close friend and right-hand man throughout his reign. In recognition of a lifetime's service to a needy king he had been rewarded personally with the earldom of Pembroke, formerly held by his wife's father, now re-created for him to transmit to his heirs, who also stood to benefit from his extensive properties in England, Wales and Ireland. Slightly at odds with King John's son and successor Henry III, but still Marshal, he died in 1219. His principal heir was his eldest son, Joan's brother William; thus at the time of Joan's marriage it was young William who was Earl of Pembroke ('second earl of the second creation') and Marshal of England.

By 1234, when Joan died, things had begun to look interesting. Although young William had married twice – his second marriage being to no less a personage than King Henry III's sister – it was all to no effect: he died, childless, in 1231. The earldom passed to his brother Richard, who also died, childless, early in the same year as Joan. The next male heir was their brother Gilbert, who now became Earl of Pembroke and Marshal of England. Gilbert was married, but he had no children and spent much of his time on horseback. His two younger brothers were also as yet childless. Now if by any chance the flow of male heirs of William Marshal should run dry, his inheritance would be divided among his daughters and their eventual offspring.

All this to explain why Dionisie de Anesty, henceforth Dionisie de Munchensi, was taking on a heavy responsibility in the shape of her two stepchildren. There was a son, John, and a daughter, named Joan after her mother. Their exact ages aren't known, but they were certainly very young – it's possible that Joan was a baby and that their mother had died in childbirth. In or about 1236 Dionisie presented Warin with a second son, who was named William.

It's possible – I signal this as guesswork, but I'm not the only one to make this guess – that Dionisie was a little out of her depth linguistically. The language of English noble families was French and no nonsense. The descendants of William Marshal were as noble as could be, and their connections were nobler still. Little John and Joan had an uncle-by-marriage, Richard of Cornwall, who was Henry III's brother and a contender for the title of Holy Roman Emperor. Their aunt Eleanor was Henry III's sister. Through these two John and Joan would be on visiting terms with the whole royal family of England, and it all spoke French.

Warin probably spoke French too, after a fashion, but medieval fathers with so many properties to run had no time for idle conversation with toddlers. Did Dionisie speak French? Not fluently, perhaps.[2] Her father started out in life as a farm manager rather than a landowner. Her mother brought land into the family, but even on that side there was no nobility, and one must look some generations back to find a French connection.

If this linguistic guess is correct, it would explain the particular value of the gift from Walter de Bibbesworth to Dionisie de Munchensi. '*Chere soer*', he begins, using a form of address that expresses a certain equality in their social status and a definite friendship between them, '*Dear sister, Since you have asked me to put in writing for your children a phrase book to teach them French, I have done this as I learned the language myself and as the expressions came back to my mind.*' Dionisie may need some help in teaching her newly acquired children French; Walter is equipped to give it. Exactly how he learned his French must again be guesswork. Some trouble might well have been taken to teach him the language of the aristocracy of which he was a modest member. His parents' marriage may have been bilingual; his family may have had

2. 'The original patroness of the work ... was by no means fully bilingual': Rothwell 1968, p. 38.

links with France that are now unknown; his father may have fought or served in the parts of France that were under English government. Walter himself was to serve there later.

He handled French fluently, but he didn't learn the language purely by immersion, if we may judge by the next clauses of his dedicatory letter: 'so that the children will know the correct names of the things they see, and will know when to say mon and ma, son and sa, la and le, moi and je.' Walter had been taught to think about the grammar of French; he knew that his distant pupils would need to think about it too. He had also learned how to compose French verse, both the rough rhyming couplets of the *Treatise* and the more complex rule-bound structure displayed in the *tençon* that he wrote in 1270 – a form typical of troubadour poetry and rare in Anglo-Norman literature.

Walter's *Treatise*, it is usually assumed, was put to its intended use. It will surely have helped Dionisie de Munchensi to teach French to John, Joan and William and to improve her own French in the process.[3] It will have made all four of them smile: it's difficult not to smile when following Walter on his self-chosen path through the maze of the medieval Anglo-French wordhoard or vocabulary.

Before returning to the *Treatise* and its unusual qualities I must complete the stories of the people around it.

In 1241, when John was about nine years old and Joan about seven, their uncle Gilbert – William Marshal's third son – was killed outright in a fall from his horse. This was so striking an event that the contemporary historian Matthew Paris sketched an illustration of it in his *Chronica Majora*. Gilbert had fathered no children; the inheritance passed to his brother Walter, who was henceforth fifth Earl of Pembroke and Marshal of England. He enjoyed these positions for four years; then he too died. He had no children either. The inheritance would next have passed to Anselm, the last of the five brothers, who, however, died six weeks later, before there was even time to invest him with the earldom. And Anselm, too, was childless.

---

3.   See Jambeck 2005. Evidently, and as Clanchy (1979, p. 225) saw, Dionisie could already read both French and English; I see no grounds to argue that she had studied Latin (ib., p. 245).

Thus on 23 December 1245 the earldom of Pembroke fell into abeyance. The genealogists began to dispute whether to count Anselm as 'sixth earl of the second creation' or not, and they are still at it. Meanwhile the lawyers set to work dividing the inheritance of the great William Marshal among his five daughters. Since Joan was dead, Joan's children, Dionisie's two stepchildren, stood to inherit what would have been her share.

Then, in 1247, young John de Munchensi died. Which at least made the lawyers' task easier: Joan's share of the inheritance no longer had to be subdivided. In this way her one surviving child, the younger Joan, Dionisie's stepdaughter, inherited a vastly more generous tranche of Marshal wealth than any of her numerous cousins, and at the age of about fifteen suddenly and unexpectedly became, without exaggeration, the most eligible heiress in the kingdom. Thanks to Walter she surely spoke good French. The only question was: who would marry her?

The question was of sufficient magnitude to be of interest to King Henry III himself, and it was he who determined the answer. It happened that in the same year 1247 the King's three half-brothers of the Lusignan family – sons of his mother, Isabelle of Angoulême, by her second marriage – had had enough of life in Poitou. Or it might be truer to say that the King of France had had enough of them. At Henry's invitation they crossed the Channel and joined his court. They were, however, landless. What could be more suitable, as a means of restoring dignity and wealth to the dashing William de Valence, eldest of the three, than marriage to Joan de Munchensi? They were married at once. 'Thus the nobility of England devolved in a large measure to unknown foreigners,' comments the historian Matthew Paris sourly, with a glance at Joan's 'very rich inheritance'.[4] From 1245 until her death in 1307 Joan was Countess of Pembroke for everyday purposes, though she never used the title;[5] her husband, sometimes in and sometimes out of royal favour, enjoyed the income and privileges that accrued to such a lady's consort. After 1307 their son Aymer took the title of Earl

4. Quoted from Richard Vaughan's translation (1993, p. 29).
5. Her surviving household accounts for 1295–1296 are a rich source for social history (see e.g. Johnstone 1929).

of Pembroke, and was prominent in the quarrels that engulfed Piers Gaveston and King Edward II.

What of the others, meanwhile? Warin de Munchensi died in 1255; Matthew Paris accounted him one of the wisest and most noble barons, 'zealous for the peace and liberty of the realm', though no one quite knows why.[6] His son by Dionisie, William de Munchensi (possibly more confident in French, thanks to Walter, than his father had been) had an eventful career in London politics, finding himself more than once in rebellion against royal authority, though never brought to trial. William's private life, too, was not unexciting. Before dawn on 24 August 1279, at the porch of Hill Croome church in Herefordshire, he married a certain Amicie at the insistence of the lady's father. Before or after this highly irregular ceremony, and certainly before 1284, he and Amicie had a daughter, who was called Dionisie after her grandmother. William died in 1287.

Meanwhile Dionisie de Munchensi, William's mother and the addressee of Walter's *Treatise*, lived on as a wealthy widow until at least 1293. In that year, by her gift, a nunnery of the order of Poor Clares was founded at Waterbeach near Cambridge. It lasted just over fifty years. In 1347 (one year before she founded Pembroke College) Mary, dowager Countess of Pembroke, Aymer's widow, endowed a wealthier abbey on the Isle of Denny near Ely, and the nuns of Waterbeach moved there.

Finally I return to Walter de Bibbesworth himself. He is known to have served around the year 1250 on the staff of the seneschal of Aquitaine, Nicholas de Molis. Apart from the *Treatise* three briefer poems by him have survived. Two of these are in praise of beauty and of the Virgin Mary, *De bone femme la bounté*[7] and *Amours m'ount si enchaunté*.[8] The third, composed in the year 1270, is a poetic argument, a *tençon*, in which Walter teases the nineteen-year-old Henry de Lacy,

6. Quoted via H. W. Ridgeway in the *Oxford Dictionary of National Biography* (2004).

7. Hunt 2004 stated that this is 'now usually attributed to Nicolas Bozon'. Rothwell in an introductory note to his online edition (2009, p. 95) explains how that attribution arises, adding that 'it is not possible to say categorically which ... is correct'.

8. Edited by Rothwell 2009, p. 99.

Earl of Lincoln, on the grounds that Walter is off on crusade while Henry, for love of a certain woman, is staying in England.[9] The author or authors of a *tençon* were not under oath, but two real facts reflected here are that the Ninth Crusade was about to take place, and that Henry de Lacy, recently married and with heavy responsibilities at home, did not go. If Walter went, he apparently survived the experience: he is said to have been buried, 'in the beginning of the reign of Edward I', at Little Dunmow in Essex.[10] He had a son, also called Walter.

In some previous adumbrations of this story there has been more than necessary vagueness about the dates. I have tried, with the help of works cited at 'Sources and interpretations', to get the dates of marriages, births and deaths as close to accuracy as can be managed. This was a useful exercise because it pins down the one occasion at which (I think) the *Treatise* must have been presented. It can hardly have been at any other date than around Dionisie's wedding to Warin de Munchensi, in 1234 or 1235. One might just stretch as far as 1241, by which time Joan was seven or older – very late to be starting a second language – and Dionisie's own son, William, was about five. I make that allowance because of the published opinion that the *Treatise* was written between 1240 and 1250,[11] but I find it less likely.[12] The suggestion has also been made that it was written when Dionisie was a widow again, after 1255[13]. That carries no conviction: by that time Joan was a married woman and William was almost twenty-one.

9.   Edited by Wright and Halliwell 1845 vol. 1, pp. 134–136, and by Thiolier-Méjean 1980.
10. Morant 1768, p. 410; W. A. Wright 1871; Hunt 2004.
11. Hunt 2004.
12. Kennedy 2003 (pp. 132–133) takes it, if I understand correctly, that the *Treatise* aimed particularly to teach French to Joan because she was to marry William de Valence. It is an attractive idea. There was, however, no long interval in which to prepare for that marriage; as shown above, it resulted from a series of events that could hardly have been predicted during Joan's childhood, followed by a rather sudden royal decision.
13. Jambeck 2005 ('widow', p. 164). Rothwell 1990 wrote that 'scholarly opinion is agreed on placing it in the second half of the thirteenth century'; this, if intended of the philologists who preceded Rothwell himself, is certainly true.

I now leave the personal context behind: the *Treatise* had a life of its own. In what follows my aim is limited (but still useful, I hope): to set it in context for readers who are not specialists in Anglo-Norman or Middle English.

There is no fixed boundary between Old French and its Anglo-Norman variant, and no boundary at all between Old French and Anglo-Norman literature. 'Anglo-Norman' is a convenient term to designate what was spoken and written in French in England (not to mention Norman-ruled Wales and Ireland). But it isn't solely a geographical thing.

The French language of William the Conqueror's followers was an extension of the French that was being spoken at the same moment in France, heavily weighted in favour of the speech of Normandy, the region from which many of them came. From that time onwards the French speech of France and England gradually differentiated. The frontier with France was far from absolute – there was plenty of interaction across the Channel – but it was real: a physical boundary, an arm of the sea that took some trouble to cross and that many people never crossed. In England the French-speaking minority – though high in status – was small and not renewed by continuing migration on any large scale. It interacted continually with the English-speaking majority. This interaction happened in public life and daily work; also within households in the context of bilingual marriages and the employment of English-speakers as servants. It was sufficient to effect significant changes in the phonology, morphology, syntax and vocabulary of the French that was being written and spoken in England. These differences from the French of France make Anglo-Norman texts easily recognizable as such.

The twelfth and thirteenth centuries were the heyday of Anglo-Norman written literature. Some genres flourished in England more luxuriantly than in France. Speakers and writers can scarcely have foreseen what was to follow. French speakers in England were too few and scattered. French was in competition not only with English but also with Latin, much used in government, church and scholarship: French was not required in sufficient everyday contexts. During the fourteenth century it ceased to be a mother tongue. Literature in English – a poor, weak tradition during those two centuries – revived and flourished in its turn, powerfully influenced by French and Anglo-Norman writings.

Thomas Wright, the first editor of the *Treatise*, was quite right to identify Walter's work as a turning point. 'This "treatise",' he wrote in 1857, 'marks a very important period in the history of the English language, as it shows that before the end of the thirteenth century, and perhaps subsequently to the barons' wars, that language had already become the mother tongue of the children of the Anglo-Norman nobility, and that they learnt it before they were taught French.'[14] On the date he was wrong: as we can now see, the *Treatise* was written shortly after the first Barons' War (1215–1217), well before the second (1264–1267); on the crucial issue, however, Wright was right (Walter would have enjoyed that). The *Treatise* is our first sign that French would cease to be one of the mother tongues of England. I return to the suggestion made earlier, that the *Treatise* was a particularly apposite gift in the event that Walter was bilingual while Dionisie was not. It was Dionisie, armed with what help the *Treatise* could give, who was to teach French to a future mainstay of the English nobility. One or at most two generations later that nobility would no longer learn French at its mother's knee; yet, paradoxically, at this period the status of French as essential equipment was still rising.[15]

Placing the *Treatise* in the linguistic spectra of Anglo-Norman and Middle English is not my task here: the work has been done, and is still being done, most fully in successive studies by William Rothwell and numerous recent papers by William Sayers.

The poem is Anglo-Norman by the simple definition that I adopt (since it was written in French in England during the medieval period). It is by Walter's intention a normalizing French text, occasionally making explicit assertions about the way French was spoken in France.

14. Later authors (e.g. Owen 1929, p. 6) agree with Wright that the *Tretiz* is aimed at children whose first language was English and whose second was to be French. Wright's use here of the term 'mother tongue' is natural but worth remark – Dionisie's children are, it seems, to learn both languages at their mother's knee.

15. Baugh 1959, p. 21; on the issue of the gradual disappearance of spoken French in medieval England see Rothwell's 1978 and 2001 papers.

Yet he betrays his Englishness throughout by spellings and word uses that smack of 'insular' French, the ever-changing Romance tongue of medieval England. He even unconsciously acquiesces in the adoption of English loanwords (*toune* 'barrel';[16] *bost* 'bost')[17] into his language. In addition he consciously slips into English for an occasional aside; most of all, he adds English glosses between the lines: handy clues for Dionisie, for her children when they began to read for themselves, and for the many future readers of the *Treatise*.

The language of the glosses is the Middle English of Walter's own milieu and that of the scribes who revised his work as they thought best. The glosses are highly variable from one manuscript to another because, in the assumptions of medieval scribes, poetic text was relatively canonical and in any case somewhat difficult to change; glosses were what scribes and readers inserted as they liked. Frequently, therefore, two or more glosses are offered for the same word in different manuscripts. This was a period during which thousands of French words were being borrowed into English through continual linguistic 'interference', that is, bilingual and cross-language communication. The glosses attached to the *Treatise* are fascinating not least because they help to show what French words had already become familiar in English and what words were as yet unfamiliar.

A reader becomes aware of the originality of the *Treatise* in successive steps. The first word '*Woman*' is unexpected. It surely marks her essential role in the process of teaching language to children; she is one of the readers who will be addressed by the poet from time to time. The first scene, imminent childbirth – not a moment at which bilingualism was relevant in real life – is a hint that the poet will trace a path through the ages and conditions of humankind;[18] if Walter planned this, his plan changed somewhat. The English glosses begin at the second line with '*enfaunter* = *to belittre*' (modern English 'give birth').

16. Rothwell 1994, p. 259.
17. This and further examples: Rothwell 1968, p. 38.
18. '... child-birth and the slavering of babies: hardly the most obvious intro-duction to a French course for boys and girls,' Rothwell commented in 1968 (p. 37).

The second direct address to the reader, '*You must tell him in French how to name his own body first of all*' (23–24), revises the expectations established thus far: the main structure, we now learn, will be a succession of named topics whose French vocabulary we are to learn (or teach) from the poem with the help of the glosses. Soon afterwards comes the first play on near-homonyms, '*Make the parting when you wash, eat the fieldfare for dinner*' (31–32): parting is *greve*, fieldfare is *grive*. Within a few more lines we have been warned to watch our spelling, '*Ruby with a b is worth more than rupie "snot" with a p*' (47–48), and brought up short by a paradox, '*Your look is kindly, but your eye is bleary*' (43–44).

By the time we reach line 120 we know what Walter has in store for us. We have been amused by a series of eight identical rhymes – a humorous variation in a poem mainly constructed in rhyming couplets – in lines that offer an unusually elaborate series of homonyms. Then comes a note from the author (107–110):

I gather these words for you and I'll tell you why:
They accord in sound, yet they discord in their variety.

Through many digressions, the first main topic, parts of the body, continues. It is followed by brief sections on internal organs, on getting dressed and on children's food. Then come extended catalogues of collective nouns for animals and of animal cries (215–290). Walter's *Treatise* is the earliest major source on this vocabulary in both Anglo-Norman and Middle English;[19] the value of these catalogues is not reduced by the fact that his humour allows him to include the braying of noisy men and the quaking of hazel in the second group and a bevy of girls alongside the bevy of herons in the first. Two brief asides give examples of polysemy (310–317: or as Walter puts it more simply, '*Now the different French words all expressed by a single English word*') and homonymy. These are followed by longer sections exemplifying the vocabulary of cereal farming, baking, flax and its use, brewing, fishing, the weather (a section that consists largely of digressions), flowers, herbs and fruit-trees, birds and wild animals, the making of a cart, the parts

19.   Indeed, the earliest in any European vernacular (Sayers 2009 b).

of a plough, the building of a house. There are occasional dry jokes: '*A snowflake goes into my mouth – it must have thought I was thirsty*' (582–583); and: '*My foot's gone to sleep, so don't anyone make a noise!*' (588–589) Humour aside, we note that the families envisaged by Walter have no small expectations. They want their children to participate in, or at least to be close and well-informed observers of ploughing and harvesting, housekeeping and domestic industries, cart-building and house-building; and to have a good knowledge of wild animals and plants; and to be able to talk about such things intelligently in two languages.

Then (the house having been built), the fire is made up and the house tidied in readiness for entertainment. This leads to the last section which, uniquely, is introduced as a report from an informant: momentarily Walter distances himself from knowledge of these interesting details (1105–1108).

> *A young man of fashion came here from a dinner*
> *And told us about the feast, how the service was arranged.*

Walter is in fact as well informed here as he is elsewhere: his terminology agrees well with recipe books and other specialized texts from the thirteenth and fourteenth centuries in Anglo-Norman and Middle English.

The *Treatise* exists in more than one version. Each version is known from several manuscripts, an indication of the enduring popularity of Walter's work.

Let's take first the version of which Trinity College, Cambridge manuscript O.2.21 (henceforth T) is an example; this manuscript is the basis of the second section of Rothwell's 2009 online edition. The text opens with the dedicatory letter from which I have already quoted, '*Dear sister …*' Then follows the first line, '*Feme ke aproche soun tens, Woman who is near her time …*' The poem has 839 lines, ending abruptly as the High Feast reaches the dessert stage.[20]

We can contrast with this the version of which Cambridge University Library manuscript Gg.1.1 (henceforth G) is an example; it forms the first section of Rothwell's 2009 edition. The text opens with a prose

---

20. The same abrupt ending occurs both in manuscript T (Rothwell 2009) and in British Library Arundel 220 (Wright 1857).

preface which was written either by Walter in the third person or by someone else: '*Le tretiz ki munseignur Gauter de Bithesweth*[21] *fist a madame Dyonise de Mountechensi pur aprise de langage*' (The language-learning handbook made by my lord Gauter de Bithesweth for madame Dyonise de Mountechensi). The preface, outlining the topics covered, is followed by the poem, which in this version is significantly longer, reaching 1140 lines.

The most significant of later versions is that in which the *Treatise*, its individual sections rearranged, and accompanied by a full Middle English translation, forms the largest section of a composite work called *Femina*. This incorporates revisions of two other pre-existing works, an anonymous short manual of polite behaviour, *Urbain le courtois*, and a collection of proverbs in Latin and Anglo-Norman by Nicolas Bozon, *Proverbes de bon enseignement*; the whole composition aims no longer to teach French to young children, but French – and the etiquette that went with it – to adolescents. The relative importance of the *Treatise* in this is shown by the fact that its first word – *Feme* in Anglo-Norman, *Femina* in Latin – gives a title to the whole. However, since the *Treatise*, in the form in which it appears in the numerous manuscripts of *Femina*, shows many signs that the details of Walter's original work have been misunderstood – substantive changes are nearly always for the worse – I have made little use of the *Femina* version here, though I have occasionally cited words from the Middle English part of it.

Returning, then, to the two earlier forms of the *Treatise*, those that appear in manuscripts T and G, we find insignificant differences between them in spelling, occasional variety in the choice of words and the form of sentences, and fairly frequent substitutions among the Middle English glosses that are inserted between the lines of the Anglo-Norman poem. The great variation in overall length between the two versions of the poem is soon explained. T is much more matter-of-fact. It gives less space to the lexical digressions, the homonyms and

21. The author's name appears in various spellings in the manuscripts. Modern writers have fixed on Bibbesworth, which agrees with some documents and is close to the modern place-name (Bibbs Hall on the Ordnance Survey map, Bibbsworth Hall in some other sources).

the almost-random images – irrelevant and often incongruous in their context – that these homonyms evoke. Not that there are none of these digressions in G, but there are far fewer of them, and they are shorter. There are still other differences, less prominent but unmistakeable. Occasional obscure phraseology in T corresponds to text that is more readily understood in G; notably, the description of the High Feast is easier to follow. While both versions at one point express a wish in the form *'please God'* (620), T mentions God only in one other passage, where the crusts cut off a loaf are to be given *'for God'*. In G he is mentioned more canonically: those crusts are to be given *'for alms'* (1056), but we are told of the spare rib that *'God took out of Adam'* (126) and we are reminded of *'the beasts that God has made'* (218). One more difference is that whereas in T the link between one main topic and the next is handled within the verse, G contains prose subheadings.

These various differences between the version represented by T and that represented by G [22] are best explained, I suggest, on the assumption that both versions stem from Walter. T, the shorter of the two, represents the text that he first wrote at Dionisie de Munchensi's request and presented to her; hence it is preserved with the dedicatory letter that accompanied it. It reproduces his first thoughts. G, the longer text, represents his more leisurely rewriting. His fascination with the French and English lexica, particularly their homonyms, was already in evidence in the T version but he gives fuller rein to this enthusiasm in the G version. [23] The dedicatory letter is absent in G; in its place comes the preface, still mentioning Dionisie and now also naming Walter, briefly explaining the origin of the *Treatise* to a general readership.

There is one other little variation. In both versions the description of the orchard ends with a poetic riddle. This is a literary form thoroughly familiar from Old English texts, rare in Old French. Walter liked them: an earlier short section of the *Treatise* is in riddling style, *'I saw a queen*

---

22. I am simplifying. Other manuscripts, not represented by modern editions, can be claimed as representing versions intermediate between these two or significantly different from both. No adequate critical edition exists.

23. Rothwell (2009, p. 96) observes that Walter's fascination for, and skill with, the French lexicon – notably its homonyms – is equally in evidence in his shorter poems.

without a king ...' (318–321).[24] T, unusually, is longer at the point where the real riddle finally appears, and includes three macaronic lines that supply the answer in both languages (see 590–597):

> *Red this redeles wat may be!*
> *Ceo est un esclarzil,*
> *En Engleys un hyysykil.*
> (Read this riddle what it may be!
> It's an esclarcil, in English an icicle.)

Dionisie didn't like riddles, perhaps. Least of all would she like to puzzle over a riddle in a language she had not fully mastered while children around her demanded the answer. In G the answer no longer appears; Walter's real preference, expressed in this revised version, was to leave his readers (young and old) guessing.

This leads to consideration of Walter's methods and aims in teaching, a subject that I will deal with only briefly because Karen Jambeck has explored it with references to earlier work. She highlights his 'remarkably sympathetic and sensitive approach to childhood' and his 'full awareness of what young children needed to learn languages'.[25] There is no threat, throughout the *Treatise*, that its readers will make mistakes (though it is admitted that others, unnamed, fall short); his tone is 'nurturing'; he builds on 'the importance of adult-child interactivity',[26] and he knows how 'language play can be employed so as to capture attention and interest and make words and expressions memorable'. Among her examples Jambeck cites Walter's section on animal cries, which children love to imitate, and his repeated experimentation with rhyme and alliteration – awareness of which, in very young children, has been shown to influence the learning of morphological patterns.[27] She might have adduced the very first sign of his awareness of this link: the revealing sentence in the dedicatory letter in which Walter promises to

24. Rothwell's 1994 paper begins with a study of this passage.
25. Classen 2005, p. 59 (introductory comments on Jambeck 2005).
26. Jambeck 2005, p. 170.
27. Jambeck 2005, pp. 167–171 citing Carlisle 2004. By contrast, Rothwell 1968, p. 38 thought that the focus on homonyms would make the *Treatise* too difficult for children.

introduce grammatical gender (*'so that the children ... will know when to say mon and ma, son and sa ...'*) and then, as if trapped by the necessity of rhyme, playfully reverses the canonical order ('*... la and le, moi and je*').

It was long ago seen as likely, by M.T. Clanchy, that the *Treatise* was for group reading – that Dionisie's children would be looking at the text as she read it aloud.[28] This is a view with which I was all the readier to agree on first approaching the *Treatise* since two other books about farming that I happen to have worked on were also intended to be read in or to a group.[29] Walter signals this even more clearly than do the writers of those texts: he sometimes explicitly addresses an adult reader ('the caregiver' as Jambeck carefully says), sometimes younger ones (the '*beaus duz enfanz, dear sweet children*' of line 215). No need, surely, to discuss whether the *Treatise* is intended for children or adults:[30] it is quite explicitly to be read and discussed in a group that consists of both together. Jambeck points out that this matches one way in which children learn to read. Walter's explicit references to spelling reinforce the suggestion that the children for whom the *Treatise* was intended were learning to read French as well as to speak it.[31]

Rothwell emphasized the focus on 'country pursuits, natural phenomena, parts of the body'. Recently Jambeck identifies a 'focus primarily on the language of estate and household management',[32] following earlier authors (Rothwell had written of 'the specialized vocabulary that [Dionisie's children] would have to master for the running of their estates once they had come of age';[33] Kennedy of the 'appropriate level of French [needed by Joan] in order to oversee her future household')[34] but

---

28. Clanchy 1979, p. 225. Rothwell (1968, p. 38) almost agreed, but not quite: 'the mother would first absorb the French vocabulary herself and then ... pass on parts of the material to her children as they sat at her knee'. Rothwell is right, too, that the verse form of the *Treatise* aids the memory.

29. Dalby 1998, pp. 25–26 ('Cato and his readers'); Dalby 2011, p. 61.

30. The *Tretiz* 'is not for beginners'; Walter 'is writing for grown people' (Rothwell 1968, p. 38).

31. Jambeck 2005, pp. 179–180.

32. Jambeck 2005, p. 159.

33. Rothwell 1982, p. 282; similarly 2001, p. 6.

34. Kennedy 2003, p. 133.

with unnecessary emphasis. Certainly French was wanted for accounting and estate management at higher levels,[35] but in truth the *Treatise* offers scant help with it.[36] If a reader set out to manage a large estate on the basis of what it teaches, the result would be micro-management. French was not the language in which in thirteenth-century England bakers, brewers, spinners, ploughmen and cart-builders discussed the details of their work with their employers.[37] By contrast, Walter himself – in the longer version of his *Treatise* – gives us this direct clue as to why his readers were to learn French: '*To be better taught in speech and not made fun of by others*' (27–28).[38] Rightly, then, Jambeck moves on from the estate management thesis to observe that Walter 'insists on the need for correct and appropriate language', appositely citing Bourdieu's concept of linguistic habitus with reference to the social advantages it can bring.[39]

The real quality of Walter's work, viewed as a teaching text, lies in its liveliness and its proximity to real life. It is because his poem offers vocabulary on the natural world and on food and its preparation that I first looked at it; this feature will surely continue to attract readers and it has been given some special attention in the commentary. Its purely linguistic interest also ensures it a continuing readership.

Its liveliness is seen in the well-controlled brevity with which each successive topic area is handled, the almost complete absence of padding (a besetting sin of medieval rhymed verse in both English and French, avoided only by the most thoughtful writers), the surprise value of the continual diversions in search of homonyms and jingles, and the humour that is in evidence throughout. These qualities, I hope, make the poem as readable in translation as a teaching text from another time and place can ever be.

---

35. *Rules of Robert Grosseteste* (Oschinsky 1971, pp. 388–389).
36. Jambeck (2005, p. 164) cites works by Christine de Pizan and Walter of Henley that emphasize the importance of estate management as a study for women as well as men; that doesn't change the fact that in Walter's *Tretiz* estate management is not the focus.
37. As Jambeck herself says (2005, pp. 166–167).
38. As quoted by Jambeck (2005, p. 168).
39. Jambeck 2005, pp. 168–169.

This is the first time that the story on pages 9–25 has been told so fully from the point of view of Dionisie, Walter and his *Treatise*, but the molecules in the structure already existed. Therefore I need not cite the numerous primary sources, mostly legal documents, which are the elements of which those molecules are built. First, however, three contemporary narrative sources.

Soon after Warin de Munchensi's first marriage to Joan, the biography of her father, the great William Marshal, was written down in Anglo-Norman verse at her brother's command. It has been published and translated as *The History of William Marshal*. This historical poem includes brief passages on the Marshal's ten children: from this we know, for example, that it was young William, after their father's death, who arranged Joan's marriage.

An obscure *Chronicle of Tintern Abbey*, of which extracts were published by William Dugdale in *Monasticon Anglicanum* (1817–1830 edition, vol. 5, pp. 270–271), takes up the story from that point; it tells of the fate of William Marshal's inheritance through the marriages and deaths of his children and grandchildren.

Several episodes of the story crop up in Matthew Paris' great work of largely contemporary history, *Chronica Majora*. A section of this has appeared in English under the title *The Illustrated Chronicles of Matthew Paris*; it includes, as briefly quoted above, comments on Joan de Munchensi's marriage to William de Valence.

Now the modern scholarship on which I have largely relied. Thomas Wright, the first editor of the *Treatise*, knew nothing of Dionisie de Anesty and supposed that Walter's work was addressed to the younger Dionisie,[40] her granddaughter. William Aldis Wright, in a brief article about the *Treatise* in *Notes and Queries* in 1871,[41] was the first to state clearly the identities of Walter de Bibbesworth and the elder Dionisie,

---

40. Though he was already aware that she had no children, which might reasonably rule her out. T. Wright 1857, p. 142.
41. W.A. Wright 1871.

but believed that the younger Dionisie was her daughter and was not quite ready to dismiss the alternative hypothesis that she was the addressee. Later authors have rightly abandoned this option.[42]

There are articles in the new *Oxford Dictionary of National Biography* on Warin and William de Munchensi and on Walter de Bibbesworth, all citing primary sources and all including some details on Dionisie. The *ODNB* also, naturally, has articles on William Marshal and his sons (but not his daughters). One can find books and papers galore about the great man himself. As to his family, an even more useful basis is an article by Hamilton Hall, 'The Marshal Pedigree', published in *Journal of the Royal Society of Antiquaries of Ireland* in 1913. When I began the hunt for Walter de Bibbesworth, Dionisie and Nicholas de Anesty, and felt the need of a safer anchorage than the Internet genealogies in which they now play their puppet roles, I found it through their incidental appearances in the rich and well-documented volumes of the *Victoria County History* for Hertfordshire.

Although most of those who have written about Walter's work have accepted W.A. Wright's identifications of Walter and of the elder Dionisie,[43] and on pages 9–25 I have taken them to be true, some scholars are less certain than others. Dionisie de Munchensi 'may have been the dedicatee', says H.W. Ridgeway cautiously (2004), while Rothwell in his 1990 edition of the text wrote that 'of Bibbesworth himself and of his patroness nothing is known for certain, in spite of conjectural identifications'. This was literally true, but the tone was misleading. No argument has been made for detaching Walter de Bibbesworth, author of the firmly dated *tençon* as well as the *Treatise*, from the one Walter de Bibbesworth who appears in documents at the right time. Women named Dionisie (modern Denise) were rarities in thirteenth-century England: there were only two Dionisies in the de Munchensi family, and only one who was a mother.

---

42. With one unlucky exception. The fourth edition of Baugh's *A History of the English Language* claimed that the *Treatise* was written 'certainly before 1250' but that it was dedicated to a Dionisie who was 'later married to one of the sons of the earl of Oxford' (Baugh and Cable 1993, p. 134) – to our younger Dionisie, born around 1280.

43. Notably the widely cited paper by Baugh 1959.

It is true that Annie Owen, the second editor of the *Treatise*, developed the thesis that it was addressed to an intermediate Dionisie, supposed to have been the elder Dionisie's daughter-in-law, William de Munchensi's wife and the stepmother of the younger Dionisie. Owen is not the only one to have accepted the existence of this ghostly figure, who had already figured in Welbore St Clair Baddeley's history of Painswick.[44] Dionisie being such a rare name, these scholars should perhaps have been less ready to believe that Walter and his son William married two unrelated Dionisies. There was in fact no such person (the supposed references to her turn out to refer to the elder Dionisie); the younger Dionisie was an only child, while the *Treatise* is expressly intended for 'children'; and, finally, it is practically certain that Walter was dead before the younger Dionisie was born.

There has recently been a view that the addressee of the book was Joan de Munchensi (Dionisie's stepdaughter) and that Dionisie was Joan's alternative name. I find no evidence in favour of this; it is probably, in origin, a slip. I cite Sayers here,[45] but unfairly: I don't think he was the first to state this view; what's more, I believed it myself briefly.

The term 'patroness' quoted from Rothwell above, and used by others, is true in a precise literary sense but it can be misleading. Yes, if we take the dedicatory letter literally – and we have no reason not to – Dionisie asked for this book; but, if we continue to take it literally, her relationship with Walter was not that of patron and client but rather one of real or assumed equality,[46] as was that of Walter and Henry de Lacy in the *tençon* of 1270. This is why I haven't followed Karen Jambeck in calling the addressee of the *Treatise* 'Madame de Mountechensy';[47] instead, taking Walter's *'Chere soer'* as a hint, I have preferred the more informal 'Dionisie'.[48]

---

44. 'There is apt, naturally, to arise some confusion here on account of the curious sequence of three Dionysias' (Baddeley 1907, p. 87): he spoke more truly than he knew. Owen 1929, pp. 40–41.
45. Sayers 2009 d, p. 51 note 2, and similarly in some of his other papers.
46. Rothwell himself recently (2009, p. 95) emphasizes Walter's high status.
47. Jambeck 2005 passim.
48. I don't go quite as far as the 'Denise' of the *Oxford Dictionary of National Biography*. My frequent citations from Jambeck, Rothwell and Sayers

THE TRANSLATION

The existence of Walter's *Treatise* was first reported in modern times by Francisque Michel in 1839 in a report of his explorations in London libraries.[49] It was first edited, from manuscript Arundel 220 in the British Museum (now the British Library), by Thomas Wright in 1857. Annie Owen in 1929 edited the text using several manuscripts; her work has been severely criticized for inaccuracy. The best modern editions are Rothwell's plain text of 1990 and his new online edition of 2009, which transcribes two manuscripts, Cambridge University Library MS Gg.1.1 (G) and Trinity College, Cambridge, MS O.2.21 (T).

I generally use the text of G, edited by Rothwell, as the basis for my translation. As explained above, I think this version represents Walter's second thoughts. I have indicated in the footnotes all significant passages that are found in this version and not in manuscript T, which I see as representing Walter's first text, the one he presented to Dionisie de Munchensi. Occasional phrases are translated from the text of T where I find it more coherent.

At the beginning and end the two manuscripts differ in a slightly complicated way. They have completely different introductory texts: G has a preface explaining to readers in general the origin and purpose of the work, while T begins with a dedicatory letter, evidently to Dionisie de Munchensi, whom Walter addresses as 'dear sister'. Both introductory texts are translated below. I have also translated both versions of the 'High Feast' with which the poem ends.

I have not given any translations from the later reworking of Walter's text known as *Femina Nova* or simply *Femina*. Where that version differs from the older ones the change is usually for the worse. In its

---

will show how much I have learned from their work on Walter and how insignificant are my occasional disagreements with them.

49. Michel 1839, pp. 47–48.

favour, however, in place of the glosses in the older versions *Femina* has a complete Middle English translation.[50]

Where there is an English gloss in the early manuscripts, I have preferred to use the same word in my translation. Sometimes more than one word is given in different manuscripts, allowing me a choice. Often, of course, I have been unable to follow this self-imposed rule because the word given in the gloss has fallen out of use in modern English and been replaced by another.

The footnotes specify most of the English glosses in the manuscripts that differ from the word used in my English translation: not quite all of them, but all those that belong to the vocabulary of farming, food and household life. The spellings in the footnotes are not always those of the manuscripts (which in any case vary), but rather those of the relevant *Oxford English Dictionary* (*OED*) entry. Wherever the difference is interesting I quote both: the manuscript spelling first, then a reference to the *OED* entry. This will make it easy to consult the *OED* for any of these words. If a word used in a gloss is not in the *OED* (or, to be more honest, if I haven't managed to find it there) it is marked +.

I refer only rarely in the footnotes to the *Middle English Dictionary* (*MED*), the *Anglo-Norman Dictionary* (*AND*) and other specialized lexicographical works, because this translation is addressed mainly to non-philologists. Let me say now, then, that nearly all the Anglo-Norman words in Walter's text, and certainly almost all of those mentioned in the footnotes, can easily and profitably be looked up in the online version of *AND* (*AND2*, to be precise). Many references to this, also to *MED* and to the major Old French dictionaries will be found in Rothwell's footnotes to his 2009 online edition of the *Tretiz*.

In the notes I use the term 'Anglo-Norman' for the language of Walter's text and of other texts in medieval French written in England. This begs a question or two, as discussed in the introduction. When I say 'Old French' I mean the medieval French of Continental texts.

---

50. Lines 1–214 in the version translated below correspond fairly closely to, pp. 11–26 of Rothwell's 2005 edition of *Femina*; lines 215–243 to, pp. 2–5; lines 244–309 to, pp. 6–11; lines 310–409 to, pp. 26–37; lines 461–1140 to, pp. 37–81.

BIBLIOGRAPHY

Paul Acker, 'An Anglo-Norman-Middle English glossary of tree and bird names', *Medium Aevum* vol. 62 (1993), pp. 285–288.

E.J. Arnould, 'Les sources de *Femina nova*', in *Studies in French Language and Mediaeval Literature Presented to Professor Mildred K. Pope* (Manchester University Press, 1939), pp. 1–9.

Thomas Austin, ed., *Two Fifteenth-century Cookery-books: Harleian MS. 279 (ab. 1430), & Harl. MS. 4016 (ab. 1450), with Extracts from Ashmole MS. 1439, Laud MS. 553, Douce MS. 55*. Oxford University Press, 1888.

Welbore St Clair Baddeley, *A Cotteswold Manor, Being the History of Painswick*. Gloucester: John Bellows, 1907.

Albert C. Baugh, 'The date of Walter of Bibbesworth's *Traité*', in *Festschrift für Walther Fischer* (Heidelberg: Winter, 1959), pp. 21–33.

—— & Thomas Cable, *A History of the English Language*. 4th ed. London: Routledge, 1993.

E.G.W. Braunholtz, 'Cambridge fragments of an Anglo-Norman *Roman de Horn*', *Modern Language Review* vol. 16 (1921), pp. 23–33.

Edmund Brock, ed., *Morte Arthure*. London: Early English Text Society (EETS), 1871.

Joanne F. Carlisle, 'Morphological processes that influence learning to read', in C. Addison Stone and others, eds., *Handbook of Language and Literacy* (New York: Guilford Press, 2004), pp. 318–339.

Michael T. Clanchy, *From Memory to Written Record: England 1066–1307*. London: Arnold, 1979.

Albrecht Classen, 'Philippe Ariès and the consequences', in A. Classen, ed., *Childhood in the Middle Ages and the Renaissance* (Berlin: De Gruyter, 2005), pp. 1–66.

Thomas Cogan, *The Haven of Health*. London: Roger Ball, 1636 (first published 1596).

Andrew Dalby, tr., *Cato: On Farming*. Totnes: Prospect Books, 1998.

——, *Dangerous Tastes: The Story of Spices*. London: British Museum, 2000.

——, tr., *Geoponika: Farm Work*. Totnes: Prospect Books, 2011.

F.J. Furnivall, ed., *Early English Meals and Manners*. London: EETS, 1868.

F. Godefroy, *Dictionnaire de l'ancienne langue française*. Paris, 1880–1902.

Renate Haas, 'Femina: female roots of "foreign" language teaching and the rise of mother-tongue ideologies', *Exemplaria* vol. 19 no. 1 (2007), pp. 139–162.

Constance B. Hieatt, '"Ore pur parler de array de une graunt mangerye": the culture of the "newe get", ca. 1285', in *Acts of Interpretation: the Text in its Contexts, 700–1600* (Norman, Oklahoma, 1982), pp. 219–233.

——, ed., *An Ordinance of Pottage*. London: Prospect Books, 1988.

—— & Sharon Butler, eds., *Curye on Inglysch*. London: Oxford University Press, 1985.

—— & R. Jones, 'Two Anglo-Norman culinary collections', *Speculum* vol. 61 (1986), pp. 859–882.

Household Ordinances and Regulations. London: Society of Antiquaries, 1790.

Tony Hunt, 'Les gloses en langue vulgaire dans les mss. de l'*Unum Omnium* de Jean de Garlande', *Revue de linguistique romane* vol. 43 (1979), pp. 162–78.

——, 'Bibbesworth, Walter of (b. in or before 1219, d. in or after 1270)', in *Oxford Dictionary of National Biography* (Oxford: Oxford University Press, 2004 and on line).

Karen Jambeck, 'The Tretiz of Walter of Bibbesworth: cultivating the vernacular', in A. Classen, ed., *Childhood in the Middle Ages and the Renaissance* (Berlin: De Gruyter, 2005), pp. 159–183.

Lisa Jefferson, 'Neville, Babthorpe and the Serjeants: three fifteenth century feast menus', *Oxoniensia* vol. 63 (1998), pp. 241–249.

Hilda Johnstone, 'Poor-relief in the royal households of thirteenth-century England', *Speculum* vol. 4 (1929), pp. 149–167 .

Kathleen Kennedy, '*Le Tretiz* of Walter of Bibbesworth', in Daniel T. Kline, ed., *Medieval Literature for Children* (New York: Routledge, 2003), pp. 131–142.

John Koch, 'Der anglonormannische Traktat des Walter von Bibbesworth in seiner Bedeutung für die Anglistic', *Anglia* vol. 58 (1934), pp. 30–77.

Andres Kristol, 'L'enseignement du français en Angleterre (XIIIe-XVe siècles): les sources manuscrites', *Romania* vol. 111 (1990), pp. 289–330.

Bruno Laurioux, 'Cuisine et médecine au Moyen Âge: alliées ou ennemies?', in *Cahiers de recherche médiévales et humanistiques* vol. 13 spécial (2006), pp. 223–238. On line at http://crm.revues.org/index862.html.

L.H. Livingston, *Skein-winding Reels: Studies in Word History and Etymology*. Ann Arbor: University of Michigan Press, 1957.

W. B. Lockwood, *The Oxford Book of British Bird Names*. Oxford: Clarendon Press, 1984.

Francisque Michel, 'Rapport', in *Collection de documents inédits sur l'histoire de France publiés par ordre du Roi* (Paris, 1839).

Frankwald Möhren, 'Onefold lexicography for a manifold problem', in D. A. Trotter, ed., *Multilingualism in Later Medieval Britain* (Cambridge: Brewer, 2000), pp. 157–168.

Philip Morant, *The History and Antiquities of the County of Essex*. 2 vols. 1763–1768.

Dorothea Oschinsky, ed., *Walter of Henley and Other Treatises on Estate Management and Accounting*. Oxford: Clarendon Press, 1971.

Annie Owen, *Le traité de Walter de Bibbesworth sur la langue française*. Paris: PUF, 1929.

H. Rosamond Parsons, 'Anglo-Norman books of courtesy and nurture', *PMLA* vol. 44 (1929), pp. 383–455.

H.W. Ridgeway, 'William de Valence and his familiares, 1247–72', *Historical Research* vol. 48 (1992), pp. 239–257.

——, 'Munchensi, Warin de (*c.* 1195–1255)', in *Oxford Dictionary of National Biography* (Oxford: Oxford University Press, 2004 and on line).

——, 'Munchensi, William de (*c.* 1235–1287)', in *Oxford Dictionary of National Biography* (Oxford: Oxford University Press, 2004 and on line).

Maxime Rodinson, 'La Ma'muniyyat en Orient et en Occident', in *Etudes d'orientalisme dédiées à la mémoire de Lévi-Provençal* (Paris: Maisonneuve et Larose, 1962); English translation by Barbara Inskip: 'Ma'muniyya East and West', in *Petits Propos Culinaires* 33 (1989), pp. 15–25; reprinted in M. Rodinson and others, *Medieval Arab Cookery* (Totnes: Prospect Books, 2001), pp. 183–197.

Michel Roché, 'Quelques noms d'oiseaux', in Marc Plénat, ed., *L'emprise du sens* (Amsterdam, 1999).

William Rothwell, 'The teaching of French in medieval England', *Modern Language Review* vol. 63 (1968), pp. 37–46.

——, 'A quelle époque a-t-on cessé de parler français en Angleterre?', in

Mélanges de philologie offerts à Charles Camproux (Montpellier: Université Paul-Valéry, 1978) vol. 2, pp. 1075–1089.

——, 'A mis-judged author and a mis-used text: Walter de Bibbesworth and his Tretiz', *Modern Language Review* vol. 77 (1982), pp. 282–293.

——, ed., *Walter of Bibbesworth: Le Tretiz*. London: Anglo-Norman Text Society, 1990. On line at http://www.anglo-norman.net/texts/bibbes-contents.html.

——, 'Of kings and queens, or nets and frogs: Anglo-French homonymics', *French Studies* vol. 48 (1994), pp. 257–273.

——, 'Anglo-French and Middle English Vocabulary in *Femina nova*', *Medium Aevum* vol. 69 (2000), pp. 34–58.

——, 'The teaching and learning of French in later medieval England', *Zeitschrift für französische Sprache und Literatur* vol. III (2001), pp. 1–18.

——, ed., *Femina (Trinity College, Cambridge MS B.14.40)*. On line 2005 at http://www.anglo-norman.net/texts/femina.pdf.

——, 'Anglo-French in rural England in the later thirteenth century: Walter of Bibbesworth's *Tretiz* and the agricultural treatises', *Vox romanica* vol. 67 (2008), pp. 100–132.

——, ed., *Walter de Bibbesworth: Le Tretiz together with two Anglo-French poems in praise of women*. On line 2009 at http://www.anglo-norman.net/texts/bibb-gt.pdf.

William Sayers, 'Anglo-Norman and Middle English terminology for spindle whorls', *ANQ* vol. 21 no. 4 (2008a), pp. 7–11.

——, 'Walking home from the fishpond: local allusion in Walter of Bibbesworth's 13 c. treatise for English housewives'. (2008b). On line (Kent Archaeology Society Online Research) at www.kentarchaeology.ac/authors/WilliamSayers.html.

——, 'Animal vocalization and human polyglossia in Walter of Bibbesworth's 13th-century domestic treatise in Anglo-Norman French and Middle English', in *Sign System Studies* (Tartu, 2009a), pp. 173–187.

——, 'Brewing ale in Walter of Bibbesworth's 13 c. French treatise for English housewives', *Studia etymologica Cracoviensia* vol. 14 (2009b), pp. 255–267.

——, 'An early set of bee-keeping words in Anglo-Norman French and Middle English', *ANQ* vol. 22 no. 1 (2009c), pp. 8–13.

——, 'Learning French in a late thirteenth-century English bake-house',

Petits Propos Culinaires 88 (2009d), pp. 35–53.

——, 'Names for the badger in multilingual medieval Britain', *ANQ* vol. 22 no. 4 (2009e), pp. 1–8.

——, '"Now the French for the properties of a plow": agrarian lexis in French and English in late 13 c. Britain', *AVISTA Forum Journal* vol. 19 no. 12 (2009f), pp. 21–27 .

——, 'Scullions, cook's knaves, and drudges', *Notes and Queries* vol. 56 (2009g), pp. 499–502.

——, '*Chough*: semantic and phonological development', *Notes and Queries* vol. 57 (2010a), pp. 169–172.

——, 'Flax and linen in Walter of Bibbesworth's 13 c. French treatise for English housewives', *Medieval Clothing and Textiles* vol. 6 (2010b), pp. 111–26.

——, 'The lexis of building in wood in bilingual medieval England', *Vernacular Architecture* vol. 41 (2010c), pp. 51–58.

——, 'A popular view of sexually transmitted disease in late thirteenth-century England', *Mediaevistik* vol. 23 (2010d).

——, 'Terminology for a late thirteenth-century British farm cart in French and English', *AVISTA Forum Journal* vol. 20 (2010e), pp. 36–43.

Walter W. Skeat, ed., 'Nominale sive Verbale', *Transactions of the Philological Society* (1906), pp. 1–50.

Leo Spitzer, 'Anglo-French etymologies', *Modern Language Notes* vol. 59 (1944), pp. 223–250.

Suzanne Thiolier-Méjean, 'Croisade et registre courtois chez les troubadours', in Jean-Marie D'Heur, Nicoletta Cherubini, eds., *Études de philologie romane et d'histoire littéraire offertes à Jules Horrent à l'occasion de son soixantième anniversaire* (Liège, 1980), pp. 295–307.

Adolf Tobler, Erhard Lommatzsch, *Altfranzösisches Wörterbuch*. Berlin, 1925–.

Richard Vaughan, tr., *The Illustrated Chronicles of Matthew Paris*. Stroud: Alan Sutton, 1993.

Thomas Wright, James Orchard Halliwell, eds., *Reliquiae antiquae*. 2 vols. London: John Russell Smith, 1845.

Thomas Wright, ed., *A Volume of Vocabularies*. London, 1857.

William Aldis Wright, 'Walter de Biblesworth', *Notes and Queries* 4th ser. Vol. 8 (1871), p. 64.

——, ed., *Femina*. London: Roxburghe Club, 1909.

DICTIONARIES CITED BY ABBREVIATED TITLES.

AND: Louise W. Stone, William Rothwell, eds., *Anglo-Norman Dictionary*. London, 1977– and on line.

MED: Hans Kurath, Sherman McAllister Kuhn, Robert E. Lewis, *Middle English Dictionary*. Ann Arbor, 1952–.

ML: W. Meyer-Lübke, *Romanisches etymologisches Wörterbuch*. Heidelberg: Winter, 1930–35.

OED: J.A. Simpson, E.S.C. Weiner, eds., *The Oxford English Dictionary*. 2nd ed. Oxford: Oxford University Press, 1989.
(In the footnotes which follow, I have replaced the *Dictionary* abbreviation 'sb.' (substantive) by 'n.' (noun).

THE TREATISE OF WALTER OF BIBBESWORTH

Preface (MS G)

Le tretiz ki munseignur Gauter de Bithesweth fistt a madame Dyonise de Mountechensi pur aprise de langage. E ço est a saver de primeretens ke home neistra ou tut le langage par sa nature en sa juvente, puis tutle frraunceis cum il encurt en age e en estate de husbondrie e manaungerie, com pur arer, rebingner, waretter, semer, searcler, syer, fauger, carier, muer, batre,ventre e mouwere, pestre, brescer, bracer, haute feste araer. Puis tut le fraunceis des bestes e desoyseaus, chescune assemblé e par sa nature apris. Puis trestuit le frraunceys des boys, preez e dé pastures, vergers, gardins, curtillages ové tut le fraunçais des flurs e des fruz qui i sunt e tut issint troverez vous le dreit ordre en parler e en respundre qe nuls gentils homme coveint saver. Dounc tut dis troverez vous primes le fraunceis e puis le engleise amount.

Dedication (MS T)

Chere soer, pur ceo ke vus me priastes ke jeo meyse en escrit pur vos enfaunz acune aprise en fraunceis en breve paroles, jeo l'ay fet souloum ce ke jeo ay apris e solum ceo ke les paroles me venent en memorie, ke les enfaunz pusent saver les propretés dé choses ke veent e kant deyvent dire moun e ma, soun e sa, la e le, e mey e ge.

Preface (University Library, Cambridge, MS Gg.1.1)

The language learning handbook made by my lord Gauter de Bibbesweth for madame Dionisie de Montchensi: specifically, from the time of a man's birth, with the whole vocabulary of his childhood; then all the French of his coming to adulthood and of his practice of husbandry and estate management, as in ploughing, re-ploughing, ploughing fallow land, weeding, hoeing, reaping, mowing, carting,[1] stacking, threshing, winnowing and grinding; kneading, malting,[2] brewing, holding a High Feast.[3] Then all the French of beasts and birds, each in its kind collected and taught; then all the French of woods, croplands and pastures, orchards, gardens, courtyards, with all the French of their flowers and fruits. Thus you will find the proper way to speak and answer that every gentleman needs to know. You will see the French first, and the English just above it.

Dedication (Trinity College, Cambridge, MS O.2.21)

Dear sister,

Since you have asked me to put in writing for your children a phrase book to teach them French, I have done this as I learned the language myself and as the expressions came back to my mind, so that the children will know the correct names of the things they see, and will know when to say *mon* and *ma*, *son* and *sa*, *la* and *le*, *moi* and *je*.

1.   Anglo-Norman *carier*, 'carry corn from the harvest field to the stackyard' (see *OED* 'carry v. 1. b').
2.   Near-homonyms: Anglo-Norman *brescer*, 'roast, malt'; *bracer* 'brew'.
3.   At Christmas, Easter, Pentecost and Assumption (*AND*).

Femme ke aproche sun teins
De enfaunter moustre seins
Quant se purveit de une ventrere
4   Qui seit avisé cunseillere.
E quant li emfez serra neez
Coveint k'il seit maylolez,
Puis en berce le cochez
8   E de une bercere vous purveez.
Le enfant comence a chatener
Einz k'il sache a peez aler.
E quant il baave de nature,
12   Pur ces dras sauver de baavure
Dites dounc a sa bercere
Ke ele lui face une baavere.
E quant comence de aler
16   De tay se veet espaluer,
E pur maine e pur blesure
Garszoun ou garce li deit suire,
Qu'il ne cece ne ne chece.
20   Ensi coveint il bone pece.
E quant il encurt a tele age
Qu'il prendre se poet a langage,
En fraunceis lui devez dire
24   Cum primes deit sun cors descrivre
Pur l'ordre aver de 'moun' e 'ma',
'Ton' e 'ta', 'soun' e 'ça', 'le' e 'la',
Qu'il en parole seit meuz apris
28   E de nul autre escharnis.
Ma teste ou moun chef:
La greve de moun chef.
Fetes la greve au laver
32   E mangez la grive au diner.

Woman who is near her time shows that she is about to give
      birth [4]
When she sends for a midwife, one who will be a careful guide.
When the child is born he must be wrapped. [5]
Then lay him in a cradle and get a nurse. [6]   8
The child begins to crawl before he can walk on his feet.
He naturally dribbles; [7] to protect his wraps from the dribble
You should tell his nurse: 'Make the child a bib.' [8]
When he starts to walk he is likely to dirty [9] himself with mud; [10]   16
In case of knocks and hurts a boy or girl must follow him
For fear he stumbles or falls: this is needed for a good while.
When he reaches the age at which he can learn to talk
You must tell him in French how to name his own body first of
      all,   24
To grasp the rules of *moun* and *ma*, *ton* and *ta*, *soun* and *ça*, *le* and *la*,
To be better taught in speech and not made fun of by others. [11]
My head (*ma teste ou moun chef*), the crown of my head
(Make the parting [12] when you wash, eat the fieldfare for dinner); [13]   32

---

4.   English gloss (verb) *belitter*.
5.   English gloss *swathe*, or (noun) *swathclut*, i.e. swaddling-cloths.
6.   English glosses *rocker, rockster*.
7.   English gloss *slaver*.
8.   English glosses *slavering clout, breast-clout, drivelling-clout*. In French 'dribble' (n.) and 'bib' are near-homonyms, *baavure* and *baavere*.
9.   English gloss *file* (see *OED* 'file v.²'), cognate with the adjective *filthy*.
10.   English glosses *clay, fen*.
11.   In manuscript T grammatical gender is mentioned in the dedication. Verses 25–28 were evidently added to the version represented by G because the dedication does not appear in that version.
12.   The same French word *greve* covers 'crown' and 'parting'. For the first sense the English gloss is *shode*; for the second, the gloss is *shed* (see *OED* 'shode; shed n.¹').
13.   Near-homonyms: Anglo-Norman *greve* 'parting', *grive* 'fieldfare, thrush' (*Turdus spp.*, esp. *T. pilaris*).

Jeo ai les cheveuz recercillez.

Moun toup, vous prie, estauchez.

En vostre chief vous avez toup,

36   E serencez de lin le toup,

En la rue juez au toup,

En la lute desrenés le toup.

Il i ad moun hanepel,

40   Moun frount e ma cervele,

Moun haterel ou mes temples.

E les mousters dist hom temples.

Vostre regarde est graciose,

44   Mes vostre eel est chaciouse.

Des eus oustés la chacie

E de nes le rupie.

Meuz vaut la rubie par .b.

48   Ki ne fet le rupie par .p.,

Car ci bource eut tant des rubies

Cum le nes ad des rupies,

Mult serreit riches de pirie

52   Qui taunt eut de la rubie.

De le oile est sauf la purnel

Si le pauper seit bon e bel.

En les pauperes sunt les cilz.

56   Amount les eus sunt les surcilz,

E ausi avez vous par reisun

Deus nariz e un tendroun.

I have curly hair;[14] please trim my foretop[15]
(You have a foretop on your head, you comb a top of flax,
You play top in the street, in a fight you win a tup).[16]
Here is my scalp,[17] my forehead and my brain,   40
My nape and my temple (and they call churches temples).[18]
Your look is kindly, but your eye is bleary;[19]
Wipe the rheum[20] from your eyes and the snot[21] from your nose
(Ruby with a *b* is worth more than *rupie* 'snot' with a *p*:   48
If a purse had as much in rubies as the nose has in snot,
The man with so many rubies would be rich in precious stones.)
The pupil of the eye[22] is safe if the eyelid is good and healthy;
On the lids are the lashes;[23] over the eyes are the brows;   56
Your nose should have two nostrils[24] and a septum,[25]

---

14. English glosses *crisp locks, crisp hair*.
15. i.e. forelock. English glosses *evese my cop* (see *OED* 'cop n.²'), *shear my top* (see *OED* 'top n.¹ I. 1. a'). The obsolete English verb *evese* 'cut the hair' is related to the noun *eaves*.
16. A tup (a ram) was the standard prize for a wrestling bout. The first three senses of Anglo-Norman *toup* were shared with Middle English *top* (see *OED* 'top n.¹ I. 1. a, I. 2. a, I. 2. b'). The fourth sense corresponded to Middle English *tup* 'ram, male sheep', but the scribe who wrote the English glosses in manuscript G did not understand the line, taking the word as *top* 'yarn' (see *OED* 'top n.² 1. a'; cf. Rothwell 2005, p. 14 note 97).
17. English glosses *brain-pan, harn-pan* (see also *OED* 'pan n.¹ 6').
18. Homonyms in Anglo-Norman and soon to be so in English (see *OED* 'temple n.²'); here, however, the gloss for the anatomical sense of Anglo-Norman *temple* is *thunwang*.
19. The paradox (surely one's look is the same as one's eye?) is emphasized by the rhyme in French, *graciouse* 'kindly' and *chaciouse* 'bleary'. For the latter, English glosses *goundy* and *+spaduous*; see *OED* 'spade n.³'.
20. English glosses *gound, +spaduing*; see *OED* 'spade n.³'.
21. English glosses *meldrop, +nose-dropping*.
22. English gloss *apple of thine eye*. 'Apple' had this meaning in English until quite recently (see *OED* 'apple n. 7. a')
23. English gloss *hairs*.
24. English glosses *thirls, nose-thirls*.
25. English gloss *gristle*.

Mes war ki la chouue
60   Ne touche vostre jouwe.
Vous avez la levere e le levere,
La livere e le livre.
La levere, c'est ke enclost les dens,
64   Le levere ki boys se tent dedeins;
La livere sert de marchaundie,
Le livere nous aprent clergie.
En la bouche amount est palet,
68   Tasterés vos chose orde ou nette.
E les dames sunt ententives
Pur bien laver lur gingives,
E l'encheisun est bien certeine
72   Ki eles le funt pur bone aleine.
Le col, la gorge e le mentoun
Dunt le fraunceis est commun.
Dedens la gorge est le gargate
76   E pluis parfunt si gist rate.
E si ad derere le wen au col
A chescune sage e au fol.

And beware the jackdaw doesn't peck your cheek.[26]
You have lip and hare, pound and book:
The lip is what encloses the teeth, the hare stays in the woods, 64
The pound serves as merchandise,[27] books teach children
    knowledge.[28]
The mouth, on the palate's[29] advice, will say if wine is good and
    clean.
Ladies are careful to wash their gums well,
And the reason is clear: they do it for sweet breath.[30] 72
The neck, the throat and the chin, for which the French is well
    known:
In the throat is the larynx,[31] and lower down lies the spleen,[32] 76
And at the back of the neck is a ligament[33] (every wise man and
    fool has one).

26. Near-homonyms: Anglo-Norman *choue* is 'jackdaw', *joue* is 'cheek'. The English
    glosses for jackdaw are *co*, *co-bird* (see *OED* 'co[1]'; chough'), cognate with the
    Anglo-Norman, which is borrowed from Frankish. See Sayers 2010a.
27. Anglo-Norman *marchaundie*, soon to be borrowed into English if it was not
    already (see *OED* 'merchandy').
28. Of these four the first two are homonyms distinguished only by gender (*la
    levere* 'lip', *le levere* 'hare') and so are the last two (*la livere* 'pound', *le livere*
    'book'). Anglo-Norman *clergie* had already been borrowed into English in
    the sense of 'knowledge, book-learning' (see *OED* 'clergy II. 5').
29. English gloss *above the mouth*. The Anglo-Norman *palet* was soon to be
    borrowed into English as an anatomical term and with its associated meaning
    'sense of taste' (see *OED* 'palate n. 1, 2').
30. English gloss *ande*. Lines 71–72 are not in manuscript T.
31. English gloss *throat-boll*.
32. Anglo-Norman *rate* apparently 'spleen' (certainly this is the meaning in
    modern French), inserted out of order to rhyme with *gargate* 'larynx'. The
    English gloss is *midred* which means 'diaphragm, midriff' according to
    OED.
33. Anglo-Norman *wen*, *vendon*. The English glosses are *faxwax*, *paxwaz* (see
    OED 'fix-fax, paxwax'). The parenthesis is for the sake of the rhyme, *col* 'neck',
    fol 'fool'. Lines 75–78 are not in manuscript T.

Desouz la launge est la fourcele,
80 'Os fourché' fraunceis l'apele.
E n'est pas mester tut a descrivere
Du fraunceis ki chescun seit dire,
Du ventre, dos ne de l'escine,
84 Espaul, bras ne la peitrine:
Mes jeo vous frai la mustreisoun
De fraunceis noun pas si commun.
En chef devant est la fontayne,
88 La sovereine levere e la suzaine.
En la buche sunt messeleres
E dens foreins, si tu les quers.
Au col avez un fossolet.
92 Desouz la lange e le filet.
Chescun orail si ad molet.
Par kakenole est cervele nest,
E pur certefier la parole
96 Conestre coveint la kakenole.
Desouz le orail est le gernoun.
A l'espaule avez blazoun.

Below the tongue is the collarbone,[34] which the French call *os*
    fourché.   80
And it's no use listing all the French words that everyone knows,
The belly,[35] back and backbone, shoulder, arm, chest;
I'll set out for you the French that's not so common.
In the first place come the fontanelle,[36] the upper and the lower lip;   88
In the mouth are the molars and the front teeth,[37] if you look for
    them;
On your neck you have a hollow;[38] under the tongue is the
    frenum;[39]
Each ear has its lobe; the brain is enclosed by a meninx,[40]
And to be sure of a man's word you must know the back of his
    head.[41]   96
Under the temple is the sideburn; in your shoulder you have a
    blade,[42]

34. Anglo-Norman *furcele*; English gloss *cannel-bone*. The meaning is not certain in either language. Compare Anglo-Norman *kanel, eskanel* 'shinbone' at line 148.
35. English gloss *womb*.
36. English gloss *molde* (see *OED* 'mould n.², head-mould¹').
37. English glosses *wang-teeth, foreteeth*.
38. English glosses *dalk, neck-hole*.
39. English glosses +*skale, fylet* (evidently already borrowed from Anglo-Norman *filet*: see *OED* 'fillet n.¹ 4. c' and Rothwell 2005, p. 17 note 127), *strynge* (see *OED* 'string n. I. 2. a').
40. English glosses *rim of the brain, rim of herns* (see *OED* 'rim n.²'), but also +*herespon*, which perhaps means '[outer] ear' (see *OED* 'ear n. III. 16. a').
41. A proverb (not in manuscript T) introduced to play on related senses of the Anglo-Norman word *kakenole* 'meninx; back of the head'. You need to know a man from all sides.
42. English gloss *shoulder-bone*.

[47]

Desouz le bras avez ascel.
100 Parmi le char gist le escel.
Desouz la mountayne surd le broil.
En bace tere ad bon soil.
Entre pledours sourt le toil.
104 Le vent de bise mult greve le oyl.
Aprés le aust si chet le foil.
Aprés gele si vient remoil.[1]
Cestes paroles ensi vous coil
108 E l'emcheisun dire vous voil
Pur meuz acorder en parlance
E descorder en variaunce.
Des espaules issent les braz.
112 Coustez ne meins ne lerrum pas,
Mes entre le bras e la mein
Si est trovéla kouue de la mein,
La paume dedeinz, la clay dehors.
116 E le poyne c'est la mein enclos.
E un poiné ki avez en mein
C'est la mein trestut plein.
E ambesdeus les meins pleins
120 En Frauncze apel hom galeins.
Kar meuz vodroie petite poiné
De gengevere bien trié
Ki ne ferroie cent galeins
124 De filaundre tut pleins.
Une coste de une costee
Adam en out Deus enosté
Quant dame Eve primes fist.[2]
128 Ne porte charge pur quei il gist.

---

1. T adds: Par deray cheet sovent duyl.
2. For 125–132 T has: Une coste de mé costez *(a rib of my side)* La premere femme *(dame Eve)* ad oustez. Par venteresse en ventre *(windoustre in womb)* Payn de fourment entre.

Under your arm an armpit [43] (and under the cart the axle; [44]
Under the hill the mist rises, in the lowland there is good soil, [45]
Strife sets in between opponents, the north wind hurts the eye,   104
After August the leaf falls, after frost comes a thaw. [46] I gather
      these words for you and I'll tell you why: [47]
They accord in sound, yet they discord in their variety.)
The arms are attached to the shoulders; let's not leave out elbows
      or hands,   112
But between the arm and the hand is found the wrist;
Palm inside, back of the hand [48] outside; we say fist when the
      hand is closed –
And a fistful when the hand is full of little things.
Both hands empty or full are called *les galeyns*. [49]   120
(A single handful of well-chosen ginger is worth more
Than a hundred double-handfuls of gossamer.)
One rib from one side [50] God took out of Adam
When he created lady Eve. It didn't matter where it was: 128

---

43. English gloss *arm-hole*.

44. Near-homonyms: Anglo-Norman *ascel* 'armpit', *escel* 'axle'. English gloss *ax-tree*.

45. Anglo-Norman *soil*, soon to be borrowed into English, but not initially in this sense (see *OED* 'soil n.¹ 8'). English gloss *earth*.

46. Manuscript T and BM Arundel 220 add another line, 'With disorder often comes sorrow'.

47. A sequence of eight (or nine) rhymes ends here.

48. Anglo-Norman *claye*, compare *OED* 'clee n., claw n.', but the English gloss here is *the back of hand*.

49. English glosses *thepsen*, *thespone*, *goupynes* (see *OED* 'gowpen, gowpenful, yepsen').

50. Homographs: Anglo-Norman *la coste* 'rib', *le costé* 'side'. Walter is careful to say 'one' not only because it accords with the legend but also because it makes the gender difference explicit. In manuscript T the text is shorter: it is 'the first woman' who takes the rib, and she is glossed *dame Eve* in English. This, I think, suggested the longer text found in manuscript G.

Nepurquant ceo mot vient en place.
Mes bon est ke l'om le fraunceis sace
De la coste quei signefie,
132   Car tote gent ne sevent mie.
Mes en le ventre est le umbile
E par desouz est le penile.
Quises e nages ou la fourchure
136   Funt grant eyse pur chivechure.
Jaumbes e genois conoissez.
N'ad mester qe voz seient tochez,
Mes jaumbes sanz genois e karrez
140   D'engeneler serreint trop rez.
Au garrez unt ore gareters
Nos garzouns e nos esquiers,
Ne mie pur estre charretters,
144   Mes pur sauver lur laniers.
En la chaunbe avez la zure,
E tant cum braoun i est ensure
De meillur force home se assure
148   Si l'eskanel seit saunz blezure.
Plaunte i ad, urtil e taloun
Dunt le fraunceis est commun,
Mes kevil de pé e kyvil de fust
152   Vodrei jeo bien qe chescun le sust.
Au pés avez les keviles.
Ne dites pas kyviles,
Kar kevil fet hom ferm ester
156   E kyvil fet li carpenter.

The word is what we need.[51] It's good for a man to know in
    French
What *la coste* means, and not everybody does know.[52]
In the belly is the navel, and below it is the pubis;[53]
The buttocks, the thighs and the cleft[54] make riding very easy.   136
Notice your legs and knees; no, you don't need to touch them,
But legs, without knees and hams, would be too stiff to kneel.
At their hams our valets and squires have garters,
Not to turn them into carters[55] but to protect their straps.[56]   144
In the leg you have a calf,[57] and with that muscle[58] certainly
A man is sure of greater strength if the shinbone is not hurt.
There is sole, toe and heel, for which the French is well known,
But the ankle of the foot and the wooden pin I want everybody to
    distinguish:[59]   152
At your feet you you have ankles. Don't call them pins:
Ankles make people stand up, but carpenters make pins.

51.   *Ne porte charge purquei il gist* is intentionally ambiguous and I try to retain
     the ambiguity with 'It didn't matter where it was'. The rib bore no weight
     and its exact position is of no interest: only the word matters to us.

52.   Lines 127–132 are not in manuscript T, which instead has an extra line here:
     'And thanks to women winnowers wheat bread gets into our bellies,' bringing
     in the false cognates *venteresse* 'female winnower', *ventre* 'belly'.

53.   English gloss *share* (see *OED* 'share n.²').

54.   English gloss *clift* (see *OED* 'cleft n. 2. a, crike'); the translation in *Femina* is
     twyste (see *OED* 'twist n.¹ I. 3. a'). Lines 137–138 are not in manuscript T.

55.   True cognates: Anglo-Norman *garez* 'hams', *gareteres* 'garters'; the latter is a
     near-homonym of *charreteres* 'carters'.

56.   In manuscripts G and T it is certainly 'straps', Anglo-Norman *lainer* (compare
     OED 'lainer, lanyard'), but Walter's meaning wasn't easy to grasp. In BL
     Arundel 220 the word is *bannere*, which usually means a 'banner' but
     alternatively perhaps a garment of some kind (see *AND*).

57.   English glosses *calf, sparlire, brawn* (see *OED* 'brawn n. 1. b'). The latter is a
     loan from Anglo-Norman, but employed in the specifically English sense 'calf
     of the leg'; hence the word is not used at this point in the Anglo-Norman
     text.

58.   Anglo-Norman *braon* 'muscle', recalling the previous English gloss *brawn*.

59.   Near-homonyms: Anglo-Norman *kevil* 'ankle', *kyvil* 'pin, peg'.

Ore pur aprise de ceo ki est dedenz le cors de homme

  Dedens le cors ad chescun hom
  Quere, foy e pomoun,
  Esplen, bouele e reynoun,
160 Estomak, veine e nerf enviroun.
  E ne ubliez ja la vescie,
  Ky au ventre fet grant aie
  Pur ceo qe urine la quiloms.
164 Ne les reynes ja ne oblioms.
  Ore n'i faut si le fel noun
  De quanqe dedenz le cors avom.
  Si avez par dehors une pel,
168 E de une beste quire apel.
  Vos avez la char e le char,
  Mes cunt regardom de eschar.
  Eschar par folur hom revilist.
172 La char par hidour en hom fremist.
  Jeo vi la char seer en char
  E de la char fere eschar.
  Mes eus par dolur ensecchisent.
176 Lé nerfs du bevour engurdisent.
  Home e femme ount la pele.
  De mort beste quir apele.
  Le clercke soune le drener apel.
180 Li prestre fest a Rome apel.
  Ore avez oy la force du cors,
  Dedeins ausi e dehors.

Now to teach you what is inside the human body:

Within each man's body is heart, liver and lung,
Spleen,[60] bowel[61] and kidney, stomach,[62] vein and sinews all
    round,   160
And don't forget the bladder which greatly eases the belly
As it urinates from time to time. And we won't forget the
    kidneys;[63]
And the gall-bladder,[64] too, must be named among the organs of
    our body.
Outside them you have a skin (if of an animal, call it hide).   168
You have flesh (and cart,[65] but guard against scorn;[66]
Foolish scorn degrades one.) One's flesh shivers[67] in terror
(I saw the flesh lying in the cart and making scorn of the flesh);[68]
My eyes are dry with soreness; the drinker's sinews swell.   176
Men and women have skin: of a dead animal call it hide
(The clerk sounds the last peal; the priest makes appeal[69] to Rome).
Now you have heard the functions of the body, both inside and
    out.

60. Anglo-Norman *esplen*; English gloss *milt*.
61. English gloss *tharm*.
62. English gloss *maw*.
63. English gloss *thighs*, a mistake.
64. English gloss *gall* (see *OED* 'gall n.¹ I. 2. a').
65. English gloss *wain*.
66. Two true homonyms differing by gender (Anglo-Norman *la char* 'flesh', *le char* 'cart') followed by a near-homonym (*eschar* 'scorn').
67. English gloss *quakes*.
68. Extended meanings of *la char*: 'corpse' (but the gloss is again *flesh*; see *OED* 'flesh n. 9') and 'earthly life'.
69. Two meanings of Anglo-Norman *apel*, which have become two different words in English, *peal, appeal*. The word is evoked by the near-homonymous verb *apele* 'call' of the previous line, rhyming with *la pele* 'the skin' of the line before.

Ore du fraunceis de nostre vesture od tut nostre autre herneis

Vestez vos dras, beaus duz enfauns.
184 Chaucez vos gauns, souleres e brais.
Mettez le chaperoun, coverez le chief.
Tachez vos botuns e derecef
De une coreie vous ceintez.
188 Ne di pas 'vous enceintez',
Kar femme est par home enceinte
E de une ceinture est ele ceinte.
De la ceinture le pendaunt
192 Passe parmi, trespase le mordaunt.
E ausi deit li hardiloun
Passer par tru de subiloun.
Si juvene enfaunt estent la main
196 Au matin vers le pain,
Une bribe dunc li donez,
Ou une lesche si plus n'avez.
Au diner li donez des ouwes.
200 Si les attirés a ses eus.
Oustés l'eschale einz q'il hume,
L'entruit ausi e le aubume,
E li donez le mouuel,
204 A home seine bon morcel.
Mes remuez la germinoun,
Mal a defire pur chescun hom.

Now the French of our clothing and other gear:

Put on your clothes, dear sweet children; pull on your gloves,
    shoes and breeches;   184
Set on your hat, cover your head; do up your buttons and after all
    this
Gird yourself with a leather belt.[70] I don't say 'make yourself
    pregnant',
Because a woman is made pregnant by a man but she is girt with
    a belt.[71]
The hanging end of the belt goes around and through the buckle,   192
And the tongue must go through a hole[72] made with an awl.[73]

[How to present bread, eggs, apples:]

If a young child stretches out his hand in the morning towards
    the bread,
Give him a lump of it, or a slice[74] if that's all you have.
For dinner give him eggs; prepare them for his use:[75]   200
For him to sup them, remove the shell, the skin and the white
And give him the yolk, a good morsel for a healthy man,
But take out the embryo,[76] hard for anyone to digest.

70. A series of Anglo-Norman imperative verbs all of which refer to dressing oneself: *vestez, chaucez, mettez, coverez, tachez, ceintez*. There are no glosses: the words explain themselves if one knows the names of the items of clothing. Evidently these are assumed to be familiar.

71. Cognates one of which has developed a special meaning: Anglo-Norman *ceinter, aceinter* 'gird oneself, put on a belt', *enceinter* 'make pregnant'. The noun *ceinture* 'belt' is again cognate with these.

72. English gloss *bore* (see *OED* 'bore n.¹ 1. a').

73. English glosses *al, nalsin* (see *OED* 'awl, alsene, elson').

74. English glosses *sziver, schivre, schyve* (see *OED* 'shiver n.², shive n.¹ 1'). The same pair (Anglo-Norman *bribe, lesche*; English *lompe, sziver*) recurs at line 300.

75. Near-homonyms (Anglo-Norman *ouwes* 'eggs', *eus* 'use').

76. English gloss *sterene* (see *OED* 'strain n.¹ 3').

Des poumes vous die ensement
208 La manere e l'affetement.
Quant poumes mangent purceo les eiment
E de dreit enfanz a reson les cleiment,
Oustez l'estiche e la parure,
212 Si lur donez la morsure.
La pepinere vous engettez
E les pepines la plauntez.

Ore le fraunceis des bestes e oyseus chescune asemblé par son
naturele langage

Beaus duz enfanz, pur ben aprendre
216 En fraunceis devez entendre
Ki de chescune manere asemblé
Des bestes ki Deus ad formé
E des oyseaus ensement
220 Coveint parler proprement.
Primes ou cerfs sunt assemblé
Une herde est apelé,
E des gruwes ausi une herde,
224 E des grives sauns .h. eerde;

In the same way I'll tell you the preparation and presenting of
    apples.   208
When they eat apples because they like them (and children are
    right to want them)
Remove the stalk and the peel and give them the flesh[77]
And throw away the core[78] and plant the pips.

Now the French of beasts and birds, each one assembled, in their
proper terms:

Dear sweet children, to learn well you must know in French   216
How to speak correctly of the beasts that God has made
And the birds likewise, each assembled in their own way.[79]
Where deer[80] are gathered they are called a herd,
Cranes also a herd, fieldfares an *erde* without the h,[81]   224

77. Anglo-Norman *morsure*, soon to be borrowed into English in the sense 'bite';
but as Rothwell observes, the word seems to be used here in the sense 'the
edible part, the flesh' (Rothwell 2009, p. 9 note 11). The translation in *Femina*
is *the body*.
78. English gloss *kolk* (see *OED* 'colk 1').
79. This passage (lines 215–220) is briefer in manuscript T, with no mention of
God. On the following two sections, the collective nouns and the animal
cries, see Sayers 2009a.
80. English gloss *harts*.
81. A 'herd of harts' is recorded in English as early as *c.* 1205, in Layamon's *Brut*
(line 305); for another citation, dated 1576, see under *OED* 'rout n.¹ I. 1. b'.
Herd is a Germanic word, native in English, also borrowed from Frankish
into French and Anglo-Norman. *Herde* and *erde* are spelling variants; they
are not distinguished in manuscript T, but the distinction seen in manuscript
G is preserved in *Femina*.

Nyé de feisauntz, cové de partriz,
Dameie des alouues, trippe de berbiz;
Harras dist hom des poleins;
228 Grant fouleie dist hom des vileins,
Soundre des porckes, sundre des esturneus,
Bovee des herouns, pipee des oyseauz,

A nye[82] of pheasants,[83] a covey[84] of partridges,[85] a hep[86] of larks, a
   trip[87] of sheep;
People talk of a haras[88] of foals and a big throng of peasants,[89]
A sounder of pigs, a *sundre*[90] of starlings, a bevy[91] of herons, a
   peep[92] of birds,

82.   For the English terms see *OED* 'nye; nide; eye n.²'. All are borrowed from
     Anglo-Norman *nyé* (which derives from Latin *nidus* 'nest').

83.   Anglo-Norman *feisaunt*, already borrowed into English as *fesaund* (see *OED*
     'pheasant').

84.   Borrowed from the Anglo-Norman *cové*.

85.   Anglo-Norman *partriz*, *perdriz*, already borrowed into English as *partrich*
     (see *OED* 'partridge').

86.   See *OED* 'heap n. 3'; for a 1290 instance of a 'hep of larks' see ib. 'lark n. 1.
     b'. The Anglo-Norman word is *dameie*, and the English translation in *Femina*
     is +*dame*. The lark, *Alauda arvensis*, is Anglo-Norman *alouue*.

87.   See *OED* 'trip n.² 2. a'; Walter gives the Anglo-Norman as *trippe*. These words
     are apparently variants of English *troop* and French *troupe*, used of soldiers as
     well as sheep.

88.   Borrowed from the Anglo-Norman *harras*.

89.   Anglo-Norman *vilein*, a word also known in English from about this date,
     but the gloss is *cherle* (see *OED* 'churl n. 3') whose meaning had developed
     from 'man' to 'serf' because of social changes resulting from the Norman
     conquest. Lines 227–228 are not in manuscript T.

90.   English *sounder* is borrowed from Anglo-Norman *soundre*, of which *sundre*
     is a spelling variant. But in English *sounder* was generally used only for wild
     boar, the corresponding terms for other pigs being *trip* (see note 87) and *drift*
     (see *OED* 'drift n. II. 7'). The starling, *Sturnus vulgaris*, is Anglo-Norman
     esturnel.

91.   'Siege' is a later English term: *OED*'s earliest citation for 'siege of herons' (and
     'siege of bitterns') is dated 1452. The Anglo-Norman word is *bovée*, source of
     English *bevy* (applied to 'a company of maidens or ladies, of roes, of quails, or
     of larks' according to *OED*). No gloss is needed in Walter's text; the English
     translation in *Femina* is *beveye*.

92.   See *OED* 'peep n.¹ II. 3'. In spite of what is said there, the English word
     appears to be borrowed from the Anglo-Norman *pipée*, which refers to the
     way little birds are caught using a musical pipe.

Route de beofs, mute des chiens,
232 Coumble de blé, soume des biens,
Masse de argent, fimere des feins,
Greile des gelins, turbe de creceles,
Luire de faucouns, luyre de puceles.
236 Mes pucele ceo set saunz juper
Les gentils faucouns aluirer.
Eschele dist home de bataille.
Foysun dist home de vif aumaille.
240 Des dames dist hom compaignie,
E des ouwes ne chaungez mie,
Car de bone franceis nient le deit.
Ly mestre baudiment l'oustreit.

Ore de la naturele noise des toutes manere des bestes

244 Ore oiez naturément
Des bestes le diversement,
Checun de eus e checune,
Solum ki sa nature doune.

A drove[93] of oxen, a mute[94] of hounds, a cumble[95] of corn, a
    sum[96] of goods,   232
A mass[97] of money, a midden[98] of hay,
A flock of hens, a spring[99] of teal,[100] a cast of falcons, a bevy of
    girls:
A girl knows how to lure the falcon-gentle without hooting.[101]
One says a body of troops, a flock of live animals;
One says a company of ladies, and also a company of geese: 240
The two go together. Why? Decide for yourself.

Now the natural voice of each kind of animal:

Now pay attention and learn the sound
Of the voice that each animal learns to make.

93. The Anglo-Norman word is *route*, whence the English collective noun *rout* (see *OED* 'rout n.[1] I. 1. b'), but the latter is used only of game and wild animals.
94. See *OED* 'mute n.[3] 1'; borrowed from the Anglo-Norman *mute*.
95. Borrowed from the Anglo-Norman *coumble*.
96. See *OED* 'seam n.[2]; some n.[3]; soum n.[1], sum n.[2]'. Of these, *seam* is an old English or West Germanic loan from Latin *sagma*, *sauma*; the other three are all borrowed from Anglo-Norman or French *somme*, deriving from the same Latin word and influenced by Latin *summa*.
97. See *OED* 'mass n.[2] 4. b'; borrowed from Anglo-Norman *masse*.
98. English gloss +*mork*. The Anglo-Norman word *fimere* means literally 'dunghill'.
99. See *OED* 'spring n.[1] IV. 15' and 'string n.[1] II. 13. b'. The Anglo-Norman word is *turbe*.
100. Teal, *Anas crecca*, is Anglo-Norman *cercele*, often confused with *crecele* 'kestrel': see Rothwell 2005, p. vii. English gloss *teles*. The equation of *cercel* and *tele* is confirmed by *St John's E.17* (Acker 1993).
101. In Anglo-Norman the collective nouns are *luire* for falcons, *luyre* for girls, spelling variants of the same word, suggesting the cognate verb *aluirer* 'lure' in the following line. English *gentle falcon* and *falcon-gentle* ('female peregrine falcon') are loan-translations of the Anglo-Norman phrase *gentil faucoun* employed by Walter. In English the word *lure* has been used for the cry with which a falcon is lured (see *OED* 'lure n.[2] 5').

248   Home parle, ourse braie
       Ki a demesure se desraie.
       Vache mugist, gruue groule,
       Leoun rougist, coudre croule,
252   Chivaul henist, alouwe chaunte,
       Columbe gerist e coke chaunte,
       Chat mimoune, cerpent cifle,
       Asne rezane, cine recifle,
256   Louwe oule, chein baie,
       E home e beste sovent afraye.
       Putois li aynel afraie.
       Gopil cleye, thesson traie
260   Quant li venour li quer praie.
       Ouwe jaungle, jars agroile,
       Ane en mareis jaroile,
       Mes il i ad jaroil e garoile.
264   La difference dire vous voile.
       Li ane jaroile en rivere
       Si hom de falcoun la quere,
       Mes devant un vile en guere
268   Afichom le garoil en tere
       Pur le barbecan defendre
       A l'assaut ke home veut rendre,

Man speaks, bear growls[102] if he is over-excited,   248
Cow lows, crane crakes,[103] lion roars, hazel quakes,[104]
Horse neighs, lark sings, dove coos,[105] cock crows,[106.]
Cat mews, snake[107] hisses,[108] ass brays,[109] swan tisses,[110]
Wolf howls,[111] dog barks[112] and often frightens man and beast,   256
Polecat[113] scares the lambs;
Fox wails, badger[114] shrieks when the huntsmen seek their prey.
Goose cackles, gander gaggles, duck[115] quacks in the marsh
(But there's quack and trap[116] and I'll tell you the difference: 264
The duck quacks in the river when a man hunts it with a falcon,
But at war in front of a city we put a trap in the ground
To defend the barbican against men's planned attack: 270

102. Anglo-Norman *braie*, which was soon to be borrowed into English and was used of various animals including man. In manuscript T bears are not mentioned, and the verb is applied to over-excited men.

103. See *OED* 'crake v.¹; creak v. I. 1'. Another English gloss is +*lounet*.

104. Anglo-Norman *coudre coule*, purely for the sake of rhyme, alliteration and nonsense. The English translation in *Femina* has *hasyl bloweth*.

105. English gloss *croaks* (see *OED* 'crook v.²., crookle v.², crood').

106. In Anglo-Norman both the lark and the cock 'sing' (*chaunte*).

107. Anglo-Norman *cerpent*. No English gloss, suggesting that the word *serpent* was already known in its general sense 'snake, reptile'. In *OED* the oldest citation is dated 1305, but Latin *serpens* occurs in the Vulgate version of the familiar Bible story in *Genesis* 3. Compare line 537, where *serpent* is immediately followed by *colure*; at that point the glossator takes it as specific and glosses it *naddre*.

108. English gloss *cisses* (see *OED* 'hiss v.; siss v.').

109. English gloss *roars*.

110. English gloss *tisseth* (see *OED* 'sizz v.; siss v.')

111. English gloss *yoll* (see *OED* 'yoll v.; yawl v.¹ I. a').

112. The Anglo-Norman is *baie*, source of English *bay*; but the English gloss is *barks*.

113. English gloss *fulimard* (see *OED* 'foumart'). Lines 268–278 are not in manuscript T.

114. English gloss *brock*. See Sayers 2009e.

115. English gloss *ende*.

116. Near-homonyms in Anglo-Norman: *jaroile* 'quacks', *garoile* 'palisade'. The English gloss for *garoile* is *trap*.

Si ki la porte n'i perde rien
272 Si.l guerreour le seet bien.
Crapaut coaule, reyne gaille,
Collure proprement regaille.
Purcel gerist, cengler releie,
276 Cheverau cherist e tor torreie.
Troye groundile quant drache quert.
Faucoun tercel le plounoun fert.
Ausint diez li geline patile
280 Quant pouné ad en gardin ou en vile,
Car de Fraunce ai tele estile
Ki geline huppé poune et patile.
E ki trop se avaunce sanz resoun
284 A la geline est compaignoun,
Ki plus se avaunce pur un eof
Ki sa arure ne fet li boef.
Berbiz baleie, dame bale,
288 Espicer prent ces mers de bale.
Par trop veiller home baal.
A sun serjaunt sa chose baille.

If the soldier has placed it properly the gate does not suffer).[117]   272
Toad crouts,[118] frog croaks, grass-snake[119] precisely hishes,
Piglet squeals,[120] boar yells, kid bleas[121] and bull bellows,[122]
Sow grunts[123] when hungry for draff,[124] tercel-falcon takes the
    diver,[125]
Likewise hen clucks[126] when she has laid, in a garden or a town,   280
Because in France I learned to say "A copped hen lays and clucks!"
One who boasts without reason is companion to the hen
Who says more about a single egg than an ox does about his
    ploughing.[127]
Ewe bleats, lady dances, grocers take their goods by the bale,   288
A man yawns[128] if awake too long and hands over to his squire.[129]

117. This digression is discussed by Möhren 2000.
118. English gloss +*crodeth* (see *OED* 'crout v.; crowd v.³').
119. Anglo-Norman equivalent of French *couleuvre*, the name of several European snake species including the grass snake *Natrix natrix* (which, if Walter is writing about England, must be the one he means). See also line 537.
120. English gloss *wineth* (see *OED* 'whine v.; whinny v.').
121. English gloss *mutters* (not in *OED* in this sense).
122. English gloss *yelleth* for both boar and bull; the Anglo-Norman words are different.
123. English gloss +*grounes* (see *OED* 'groin v.¹ 1), borrowed from Anglo-Norman though not exactly matching Walter's *groundile*.
124. Although close in sense and sound, English *draff* (Germanic?) and Anglo-Norman *drache* (French *drêche*; Celtic?) are apparently not related. The related French forms *drège* and *dragée*, with the same meaning, were soon to be borrowed into English (see *OED* 'dredge n.² 2.').
125. English gloss *ducker*.
126. English gloss *kakeles*: I write 'clucks' here in the translation because I used 'cackles' above for geese.
127. English gloss *earing* (see *OED* 'ear v.¹').
128. English gloss *gone* (see *OED* 'gane v.').
129. A sequence of five homonyms or near-homonyms (Anglo-Norman *baleie* 'bleats', *bale* 'dances', *bale* 'sack, bale', *baal* 'yawns', *baille* 'hands over').

Aprés dormer hom se espreche.
292 Le prestre en le eglise preche.
Li peschour en viver pesche
Ore de sa rey, ore de son hesche.
Faily lest sa tere fresche
296 Pur achater sa char freische.
Quant povre femme mene la tresche,
Plus la vaudreit en mein la besche,
Car el n'ad ou se abesche
300 De payn ne a bribe ne a lesche.
Soun chael la paele lesche.
Ore donez a chael a flater
Ki lesche la rosé del herber.
304 Eschuez flatour ki seet flater
E les genz espeluper.
En tun chaperoun ne veut lesser
Un poyton, tant ad cher
308 Noun pas tei, mes tun aveir
Ke desire de tei aver.

After sleep he stretches;[130] if he's a priest, he preaches[131] in church;
If he's a fisherman he fishes in the river, now with his net, now
    with his bait:[132]
He fails to work his fallow field, preferring to buy his meat fresh[133]
While his wife leads the ring-dance.[134] She ought to have a spade   296
    in her hand
Because to feed herself she hasn't a slice of wheat bread;
Her pup licks the pan[135] –
So give the pup something to lap: he's licking the dew in the
    meadow.
Avoid the flatterer who knows how to flatter[136] and to pluck[137]
And won't leave a berry in your hood,[138] because he loves   304
Not you but your property which he wants to have[139] from you.

130. Continuing the idea of the previous line. English gloss *raxes him, rakslet* (see *OED* 'rax v., rask v.', though these are given as intransitive verbs, not reflexives).

131. False cognates, Anglo-Norman *espreche* 'yawns', *presche* 'preaches', followed by the near-homonym *pesche* 'fishes'.

132. English glosses *hock* (see *OED* 'hock n.⁵') and *hook*. The Anglo-Norman word and the two English glosses approach the same act from three aspects: the bait, the rod and the hook.

133. Two meanings of Anglo-Norman *fresche*, 'fallow land', 'fresh'.

134. Anglo-Norman *tresche*, the *tripudium* of John of Garlande. English gloss *ring*: see *OED* 'ring n.¹ III. 10. b *lead the ring*', linked with *ringleader*.

135. A sequence of 11 rhymes ends here.

136. Homonyms, Anglo-Norman *flater* 'lick' and 'flatter', and the cognate *flatour* 'flatterer'. English *flatter* (see *OED* 'flatter v.¹'), borrowed or adapted to the Anglo-Norman word, was not yet in use; hence the English gloss is *losenge* (see *OED* 'losenge v.'), another French loanword.

137. English glosses *pick, glean*.

138. The Anglo-Norman *poiton* means literally a small wild fruit but usually occurs in negative phrases, meaning 'not a jot, not a bit'. English *not a button* (see *OED* 'button n. 1. b.'), borrowed from the Anglo-Norman, was not yet in use; hence the English gloss here is *mote* (for *not a mote* see *OED* 'mote n.¹ 1. c.').

139. *Aveir* 'property' and *aver* 'to have' are the same word in Anglo-Norman (cf. modern French *avoir*).

Ore de diverseté de fraunceiz ki tut est dist de un engleis

Veez, ci veint devant vous
Un chivaler bieau tut rous
312   Qui une destrere sor se est munté.
Esku de goules ad porté,
Un launce rouge en l'uyn mein,
De vin vermaille l'autre plein,
316   Qi ne manjuwe point de peschoun
Si de le haranc sor noun.
Je vie une reyne sanz rey
Pur une reyne fere desray
320   Ki enmye le reume le rey
En un reoun sist en un rey.
Un vilein vint en ma forer
Ki eins oy foreiner
324   E dist qu'il voleit foreir,
Li lers qui vint forveier.

Now the different French words all expressed by a single English word:

> Look! Here in front of you comes a handsome knight, all red-
>   haired,
> Mounted on a sorrel charger; he bears a shield gules,   312
> In one hand a red lance, the other full of red wine,[140]
> And he eats no fish except red herring.[141]

[And some French words of similar sound:]

> I saw a queen without a king, distressed about a frog
> That sat by itself in the middle of the king's kingdom in a ditch.[142]   320
> A peasant came to my field-edge[143] who is a stranger there
> And said he wanted to search there for the thief he saw straying.[144]

---

140. *Rous, sor, goules, rouge, vermeyl*: five Anglo-Norman words which could all be translated by English 'red'; *gules* and *sorrel*, borrowed from Anglo-Norman, came into use in later Middle English.

141. When used of a horse, above, *sor* means literally 'red' (cf. English *sorrel*), but in the Anglo-Norman phrase *haranc sor* the word has a different origin and means 'salted, pickled' (cf. English *sour*). Yet it can still be translated by English 'red' in the expression *red herring*, which (apart from the glosses to Walter's text) is first recorded *c.* 1420 (in a recipe in *Liber Cocorum* in which white herrings are to be alternated with smoked herrings). And yet smoked herrings are not really red. Walter provides evidence that the expression was already in use in his time, was borrowed from French, and resulted from folk etymology.

142. Two series of near-homonyms, linked etymologically: Anglo-Norman *reyne* 'queen', 'frog', *reume* 'kingdom', *reoun* 'ditch'; *rey* 'king', 'furrow'; and the false cognate *desray* 'distress'. On this passage see Rothwell 1994.

143. English gloss *hevede londe* (see *OED* 'headland 1').

144. Four near-homonyms: Anglo-Norman *forere* 'field-edge', *foreiner* 'stranger, foreigner', *foreir* 'search, forage', *forveier* 'stray'. Translated from manuscript G; evidently a revised version of the less cogent text in manuscript T.

Ore le fraunceis du pré e du chaumpe e de carier les blez

Ore aloms as prés e as champs
Pur enformer vos enfaunz.
328   De faus fauchez un andenne de pré.
De faucil siez un javele de blé.
Les javeles en garbes liez.
En trosseaus les garbes mettez.
332   Un warrott de peis suz arascez
E les favots du warrott liez.
Mes n'ad mester ke vous dioms
De tute manere de blé les nouns,
336   De segle, orge ne forment,
Ke commune sunt a tote gent.
Mes de autre semail trop i crest
Ki pur mei a dire ne est.
340   Le yverai i crest e le betel,
Le azoun ausi e le neel,

Now the French of meadows and fields and carting corn:

> Now let's go to the meadows and fields to teach our children
> French.
> With a scythe you mow a swathe of meadow, with a sickle[145] you   328
> reap a rip[146] of corn,
> You tie the rips in sheaves and you put the sheaves in a truss.[147]
> You pull up the stems[148] of peas and you tie together the pods[149]   332
> from the stem.
> Now I need not tell you the names of all kinds of corn,
> Of rye, barley and wheat, because they are familiar to all,   336
> And too many other seeds grow for me to be able to tell them all:
> Darnel[150] grows and drawk,[151] tare[152] and cockle,[153]   340

145. Three cognates in Anglo-Norman, *faux* 'scythe', *faucher* 'mow', *faucil* 'sickle'.
146. Probable cognates in English (see *OED* 'reap v.; rip n.²').
147. Anglo-Norman *trussel*; the English is borrowed from the cognate form *trusse*.
148. Anglo-Norman *warrot*; English gloss *ris*. The sense 'stem of peas or beans' is known to *OED* only in 19th-century East Anglian dialect (see *OED* 'rice n.¹ 2. b').
149. Anglo-Norman *favat* 'pea or bean pod', misunderstood as *bean* by the glossator.
150. *Lolium temulentum*, Anglo-Norman *yverai*. Lines 334–345 are not in manuscript T.
151. *Bromus secalinus*, Anglo-Norman *betel* (otherwise unknown); also known in English as 'cheat' and 'chess' (see *OED* 'tare n.¹, cheat n.¹ 9, cheat n.², chess n.³').
152. *Vicia spp.*, Anglo-Norman *azoun* (otherwise unknown); English gloss *thar* (see *OED* 'tare n.¹').
153. *Agrostemma githago*, Anglo-Norman *neel*, English gloss *kokil*. These names were sometimes applied to *Nigella sativa* (see *OED* 'cockle n.¹' and Rothwell 2009, p. 16 note 2) but it is clear that corn-cockle is intended here.

Le blaverole e le mauwe ausi,
Caroil e autre qe ne vous die,
344 Car trop avereit trop a fere
Si tuz semaus vous dei retrere.
Mes quant tens est de carier,
Vos charettez fetes charger.
348 Mes chivaus deit li charetter
De sa riote demener.
En grange vos blez muez,
Dehors la grange vos blez tassez,
352 Car une moye est dit en grange
E une thase dehors la grange.
Moiloun apellez ceo qe est en feyn,
E thas dist hom ceo qe est en grein.
356 En graunge gardez vous des arestez,
En chaumpe vos blez des autre bestes.
En sale chauntez vous lé gestes
Pur oblier grefs e molestes.
360 Au muster verrez degysé testes
Ke resemblent cornu bestes,
Mes si vous quillez genz a festes,
Priez ceuz que sunt en questes
364 Pur lur malicez, qe sunt si prestes
De fere grevaunces e molestes.
Mes si devisé point ne estes
A ceuz donez les chars restes.

Cornflower[154] and mallow[155] too, charlock[156] and others I won't
    mention,

Because I would have far too much to do if I had to list all the   344
    seeds for you,

But when it's carting time you must load up your carts.

The carter must control [your] horses with his switch.[157]

Rick[158] your corn in the barn, stack your corn outside the barn,

Because it's called a rick inside and a stack outside;   352

Call it a cock[159] when it's hay and a heap when it's grain.

In the barn take care of awns,[160] in the field guard your corn from
    animals,

In church you'll see covered heads looking like horned beasts,[161]   360

In the hall, sing epics[162] to forget sorrow and trouble;

I suggest you invite to your feasts people who are in lawsuits

For their mischief, the ones so ready to make grief and trouble,

And you are not compelled to give them the leftover meat![163]

154. *Centaurea cyanus*, Anglo-Norman *blaverole*; English gloss *bloweth* (cf. *OED* 'bluet 2; bluebottle 1. a'), borrowed from the cognate *bleuet*.

155. *Malva spp.*, Anglo-Norman *mauwe*, English gloss *malve*, a form influenced by French that was not destined to survive in English (Old English *mealuwe*, modern *mallow*).

156. *Sinapis arvensis*, English gloss *szerlok*. The Anglo-Norman is *caroil* (and in other texts *cariloc, cherloc*), which is cognate with the English, not with any French word (Rothwell 2009, p. 16 notes 8–9).

157. English gloss *haling wippe* (cf. *OED* 'haul v. 1. e; whip n. I. 2. a').

158. English gloss *mouwe* (see *OED* 'mow v.²').

159. The English gloss *reke* is applied both to Anglo-Norman *moye* ('mow', 'rick') and to *moiloun* ('haycock').

160. English glosses *anenes, eyles* (see *OED* 'awn n.; ail n.²').

161. Cowled monks (Rothwell 2009, p. 16 note 22 and p. 66 note 16).

162. Anglo-Norman *geste*; no need for a gloss because the word was already familiar in English (see *OED* 'jest n. 1–2') . It soon lost this serious sense as the popularity of epics, *chansons de geste*, declined.

163. Last of a sequence of ten rhymes, from *arestes* 'awns' to *restes* 'leftover'.

Ore pur pestre vostre pain au fourn le fraunceis

368   Quant vestre blé est ben batu,
        Puis ventez e puis molu,
        Mes pur plus parfitement
        Parler devaunt bone gent
372   Il ad suffler, venter e corneer
        Dunt la resoun fet a saver.
        Le fu suffle li quistroun,
        E le vent vente parmi le busschoun,
376   Mes venour proprement corneie
        Quant chace prent de pure preihe.
        Mes par le moudre devent farin
        Ceo qi en greine fust huy matyn,
380   E de farine ja deveint flour
        Par le bulenge le pestour.
        Car par le bulenge est severé
        La flour en fourfre einz demoré.
384   A vos chivaus le fourfre donez.
        Eauwe teve a la flour medlez
        E vostre paste ensint pestrez,
        E de un rastuer la auge moundez.
388   Mes il i ad raster e rastuer
        Ki servent de diverse mester.
        Li pestour ad en mein la rastel,
        Mes li rastuer fest li auge bel.

Now to oven-bake your bread the French way:

> When your wheat is well threshed, then winnowed and ground   368
>
> But to speak more correctly before respectable people
>
> There is blow, winnow and wind and their meanings must be kept
> in mind:
>
> The scullion blows the fire, the wind winnows the bush,
>
> But hunters wind their horns when in pursuit of their prey[164]   376
>
> What was grain in the morning becomes meal[165] by grinding,[166]
>
> And from meal comes flour[167] through the miller's bolting-
> cloth[168]
>
> Because, using the bolting-cloth, flour is separated from the bran
> that was in it;
>
> Give the bran to your horses. Mix warm water with the flour   384
>
> And knead your dough, clean the trough with a dough-rib[169] –
>
> But rake and rib serve different purposes:
>
> The baker holds an oven-rake,[170] but the rib cleans the trough

164. Three Anglo-Norman verbs, *suffler, venter, corneer*, all related in meaning to the noun *vent* 'wind'. English *winnow* and *wind* are related, as are the corresponding Anglo-Norman *venter* and *vent*, but no English wordplay can match the Anglo-Norman *le vent vente* 'the wind blows'. Lines 370–377 are not in manuscript T.

165. *OED* 'meal n.¹ I. a.'; but the precise sense here, of a product containing bran as well as flour, is not specified in *OED*. On the baking terminology see Sayers 2009d.

166. English gloss *grist* (see *OED* 'grist v.²').

167. Anglo-Norman *flur* (clearly originating from the Old French phrase *flor de farine* 'fine flour', though this is not found in earlier texts) is the direct source of the English word *flour*. Although they are 'the same word', Anglo-Norman *le flur* is glossed as *the flour* in manuscript T.

168. In Anglo-Norman the bolting-cloth is a *boulenge* and the man who uses it a *boulenger*.

169. English glosses *dourib* (see *OED* 'dough n. 5. dough-rib') *ribbe* (see the tentative *OED* entry 'ribber 2'), +*trowhryb* (i.e. trough-rib).

170. Having suggested two cognates in the previous lines, Walter adds a third in manuscript G: *li raster* or *li rastel* 'rake', *li rastuer* 'scraper', *la rastel* 'oven-rake'.

392 Car quant le paste a auge aerd,
   Li rastuer de ceo lur cert,
   E tant cum feins sunt en prés
   Est li rastel sovent manez.
396 Eschauffez le fourn de feugere
   Pur defaute de littere.
   Littere e littere sunt divers,
   Discordaunt dient ces clers.
400 Li faucheour littere fauche.
   Pur eise en littere hom chivauche.
   Littere proprement sanz faille
   En pure fraunçé dist hom 'paile'.
404 Pail e paille sunt nomez
   Quant du greine sunt severez.
   E si paile ne seit pas,
   Pernez dunc le pesaz.
408 E quant le forn est bien chauffé,
   Du pel seit le past entré.

Ore le fraunceis de ceo ki a bone mesnere apent

   Quant le past est au four
   E de pestre i prent sojour,
412 Endemesters la mesner
   Ne serra pas trop nunchaler,
   Einz devendra bone curteller.
   Ore alez semer vostre lyneis,
416 E ne ubliez ja vostre canois,
   Car de lyn averez les bucheaus
   E de caumbre les cordeaus.

Because when the dough sticks to the trough the dough-rib   392
     removes it;
As long as there's hay in the meadow the rake will be used.
Heat up the oven with ferns if there's no straw
(But there's litter and litter, different, so bookmen say:
The mower in the meadow mows litter; a man rides in a litter for   400
     comfort.
But [the first] litter in pure French is properly called *paille*
     'straw'.[171]
Chaff and straw are so called when separated from the grain)[172]
If there's no straw, take pea-straw instead;[173]
And when the oven is well warmed, put the dough into it on a   408
     shovel.[174]

Now the French of everything that belongs to good household
management:

When the dough's in the oven and she takes a rest from kneading
Meanwhile the housewife will not be too idle,
But will turn into a good gardener.
Sow your linseed here and your hempseed there,   416

171. Two senses of the same Anglo-Norman word *littere*, 'straw', 'travelling litter'.
     The word was borrowed into English, in Walter's time or soon after, with
     both these senses (see *OED* 'litter n. 2., 3.'). Walter's claim is that *littiere* was
     not used in the sense 'straw' in the French of France.
172. As Sayers explains, Walter 'makes a distinction between *pail* and *paille*,
     glossing the one chaff (*chaf*) in English and the other straw (*stre*), but there
     is no other textual evidence for *pail* in French ... however reasonable we may
     find the distinction between the useless chaff and more valuable straw that
     results from threshing' (Sayers 2009f).
173. English gloss *pese stre* (see *OED* 'pease n. B. 5').
174. I quote Sayers once more: 'the tool used here, *pel*, the peel of modern
     pizza-bakers, was a shovel-like instrument with a long handle. Reflected in
     modern French *pelle* 'shovel', it derives from Latin *patella*. Despite modern
     English *peel, pel* is not attested with this meaning in Middle English' (Sayers
     2009d).

Vostre lyn par tens sarclez
420   E par tens le arascez.
Puis aprés la rehaez
E puis ou solail le secchez.
E pur tut sauver, mult fest bel,
424   Uncore coveint seir au pessel
Pur escuger vostre lyn,
Car autrement n'est pas fin.
E jeo requer, dame Muriel,
428   Ore vous devez au pessel.
Mes quant au pessel ad sun dever,
Dunc irrez a rastuer,
E la serence dunc pernez
432   E vostre lyn serencez.
E de un conoil vous purveez,
Mes le fusil ja ne ubliez,
E le virel ki a ceo suffist.
436   Ne sai ki plus vous serreit dist.
Mes ci ad diverseté
Dunt chescun n'est mie avisé.
De treys choses seert le fusil.
440   Le fil est filé du fusil,
E le fu de cailloun fert le fusil,
E le blé est molu par le fusil.

So that you'll have bolls[175] of flax and ropes of hemp.
Weed your flax sometimes and pull it sometimes,
Then afterwards ret[176] it and dry it in the sun
And to save it all properly it is correct to scrape with a
    swinglestick[177]   424
To scutch[178] your flax, because otherwise it won't be clean.
And I beg you, mistress Muriel, to take to your swinglestock
A good wooden stick[179] to swingle your flax
And then the hackle[180] to hackle your flax.[181]   432
Then arm yourself with a distaff[182] and don't forget the spindle
And the whorl[183] that fits it. You don't know what's coming next:
There's a distinction that not everyone is aware of,
Because a *fusil* has three uses: yarn is spun with the spindle,   440
Steel[184] strikes fire on flint, corn is ground using the mill-
    spindle.[185]

175. English glosses *bolles* (see *OED* 'boll n.¹ 3.'), +*hep*. On the flax terminology see Sayers 2010b.

176. English glosses *ret, raite, rote, rekke* (see *OED* 'ret v.²; rot v. 4. c.'), *water*.

177. English gloss *swinglestock*. Lines 423–426 are not in manuscript T.

178. Anglo-Norman *escuger*, direct source of English *scutch*. English glosses *swingle, scoche* (see *OED* 'swingle v.¹, scutch v.¹ 1.').

179. In manuscript G the Anglo-Norman term is *rastuer*, the same word as is translated 'dough-rib' above, and the English gloss is again *ribbe* (see *OED* 'rib n.³'). The equivalence is confirmed by the *Nominale* of *c.* 1340 (Skeat 1906): *Rastel, martel, et rastuere: Rake, hamur, and ribbe.*

180. English gloss *hechele* (see *OED* 'hackle n. I. 1. a.; heckle n. 1.; hatchel n.').

181. English gloss *hechelet* (see *OED* 'hackle v. 3. a.; heckle v. 1.; hatchel v. 1. a.').

182. English gloss *rocche* (see *OED* 'rock n.²').

183. English gloss *werne* or *werve* (see *OED* 'wharve n.'). Lines 435–438 are not in manuscript T.

184. English gloss *virhirne* (see *OED* 'fire-iron').

185. Homonyms in Anglo-Norman, *fusil* 'steel of tinderbox', *fusil* 'spindle'. They were not homonyms in Old French (*foisil, fusil* 'steel'; *fuisel* 'spindle'). *Fusil* 'spindle' is used here in two senses both of which correspond to English spindle (see *OED* 'spindle n. 1., 6.; mill n.¹ 11. mill-spindle'). Thus *fusil* serves as a rhyme word four times. See also Livingston 1957; Sayers 2008a.

Quant vostre fil est bien filee,
444 E vostre fusil tut emplee,
Au travil coveint dunc aler
Vostre fileie traviller.
E puis coveint a la voidere,
448 Cum du filleie est la manere
Pur voider aprés le travil.
E puis aprés tistrer le voil.
Mes quei fest ore madame Hude?
452 Un lussel de ses voiders wude.
E la tistresce quant perulé ha
Tantost ses trames voidra.[3]
E pur estre saunz blame
456 Purveier coveint de une lame.
Autre chose isi apent,
Mes ne sai verrement.

Ore le fraunceis pur breser brece e bracer cerveise

Puis ki desore suffist
460 Le fraunceis qe vous ai dist,
Ore ferreit bien a saver
Cum l'en deit breser e bracer
A la manere ke hom fest serveise
464 Pur fere nos noces bien a ese.

3. For 453–454 T has: E dit, 'Hore jeo wuyl Ma filee mettre en trahuil *(to yern
o the reel)*. Les tremes *(the spoles)* fray appariller A la tistresse pur tistrer *(to
weve)*.

When your yarn is well spun and your spindle well filled
You must turn to the reel to reel[186] your yarn,
And then to the bobbin,[187] since the custom is to   448
Wind the yarn off the reel, and then weave what you will –
What's mistress Hude doing? She's wound[188] a skein[189] from her
    bobbin
And says: 'Now I'll put my yarn on the reel:[190]
I'll get the spools ready for the weaver to weave   456
And to do it correctly I've prepared a slay.'[191]
There was more to this, but I don't truly know it,
And the French I have told you is enough for now:

Now the French for roasting malt and brewing ale:

Now it would be as well to know how to malt and brew[192]
As when ale is made to enliven our wedding feast.   464

186. Anglo-Norman *travil* (noun; Rothwell 2009, p. 20 note 7) and *traviller*
(verb); English gloss *relend* (see *OED* 'reel v.²'). Lines 443–450 are not in
manuscript T.

187. Anglo-Norman *voider, vauder*; English gloss *yarnewynde* (see *OED* 'garnwin,
garnwindle, yarnwind, yarnwindle'); Latin *girgillum* (*Dictionarius* 65).

188. Anglo-Norman *guinder, winder*, borrowed from English or Norse; English
wind (see *OED* 'wind v.¹ 15.').

189. Or ball; English gloss *clew*.

190. English gloss *werpen* (see *OED* 'warp v. III. 20. b.').

191. Or reed; English gloss +*webbing szaly* (see *OED* 'slay n.'). The preceding
lines are translated from manuscript T, which is longer at this point by one
couplet than manuscript G, but is thereafter briefer.

192. Near-homonyms in Anglo-Norman, *bracer* 'brew' (ale); *breser* 'bruise, malt'.
In both cases the Anglo-Norman words resemble the English but they have
different histories. *Bracer* came to French and Anglo-Norman from Celtic by
way of the Latin of Gaul, while *brew* is an English word of Germanic origin.
For *breser* the English gloss is identical, *breser*, and there was indeed some
coalescence between the Anglo-Norman and English words (see *OED* 'bruise
v.' and compare 'bree n.² 2.'). On this section see Sayers 2009b.

Allumés, auncele, une frenole.

Quant averas mangé de kakenole,[4]

En une cuve large e leez

468　Cel orge la enfondrez,

E quant il est bien enfondré,

E le eauwe seit descouelé,

Mountez dunc cele haut soler,

472　Si le facez bien baler,

E la coucherez vostre blé

Taunt cum seit bien germee,

E de cele houre apeleras

476　Breez qe einz blé nomaz.

Le breez de vostre mein movez

En mounceus ou en rengez,

E puis le portés en une corbail

480　Pur enseccher au torrail,

Car corbail ou corbailloun

Vos servirunt tut la foisoun.

Puis serra le brez molu

484　E de eauwe chaude bien enbu.

Si le lessez descoure ataunt

Hors de keverel meintenaunt,

Taunt cum la bresceresce entent

488　Ki ele eit bersil a talent.

E puis le berzize prendra

De forment ou orge ki ele a,

E par le geeste e le berzille

492　Dunt home plus se sutille

Par dreit dever de bracerye.

Mes tut diviser ne sai jeo mie,

Mes tut issint de art en art

496　Attirez chescune part

Deskes vous eez bone serveise,

Dount home devient si ben a eise

4.　T has: E kaunt averas mangé du brachole *(a kake with spices)*.

Girl, light a fennel-stalk[193] (after eating some spice-cake);[194]
Soak this barley in a deep, wide tub,
And when it's well soaked and the water is poured off,
Go up to that high loft, have it well swept,   472
And lay your grain there till it's well sprouted;[195]
What you used to call grain you call malt from now on.
Move the malt with your hands into heaps or rows
And then take it in a basket[196] to roast in the kiln;   480
Baskets, big or little, will serve you in plenty.
When the malt is ground and well steeped in hot water;
You let it drain sufficiently, now outside the mash-tub,[197]
Until the breweress knows she has enough wort;   488
Then she'll take the grout[198] that she has, of wheat or barley.
Thus with the barm and wort that people use so cleverly
In the proper process of brewing – I can't describe it all –
From skill to skill you must perform each process   496
Until you have good ale and people are so pleased with it

---

193. Anglo-Norman *frenole*; English gloss *kex*, a dry stalk of cow-parsley or other umbellifer used to carry fire.
194. In manuscript T the cake baked under the ashes (*bracole*), *a kake with spices* according to the English gloss, is fetched in for the rhyme. In Gg.1.1 this is reworked: Anglo-Norman *kakenole* replaces *bracole*. However, unless Walter knew cakes that we don't, the real name was not *kakenole* but *kuskenole*, a pastry turnover with dried fruit filling. There is a detailed recipe for the latter in *Coment l'en deit fere viande e claree* (text and translation in Hieatt and Jones 1986, pp. 865, 876); also a version in Middle English ('*A mete that is ycleped cuskynoles*') in *Diversa Cibaria* (Hieatt and Butler 1985, p. 45).
195. English gloss *spired* (see *OED* 'spire v.[1] 1.').
196. English gloss *lepe* (see *OED* 'leap n.[2] a.').
197. English gloss *mahissing fate, meisshing fat*, i.e. 'mashing-vat'.
198. Anglo-Norman *berzize*, English gloss *grout*; here it seems to be barley or wheat 'used as a flavouring for ale before the introduction of hops', rather as suggested in *OED* ('grout n.[1] 2. b.'). Lines 485–500 are not in manuscript T.

Ki les uns en pernent taunt
500   Ke il enyverent meintenant.
Serveise fet miracles e merveilles.
De une chaundaile deus chaundailes.
Yveresce tent lais home a clerke.
504   Home mesconnu fet aver merke.
Yveresce fet hom fort chatoner.
Home aroé fet haut juper.
Yveresce fet coyfe de bricoun
508   Rouge teint saunz vermeilloun,
E dunc dist home ki par seint Jorge
Trop ad il bu grece de orge.
A teles li auctour se repose,
512   Car parler veut de autre chose.

Ore pur peschour en vivere ou en estauncke le fraunceis

Si saver voillez la manere
Cum pescher devez en vivere,
Vivere est proprement nomé
516   Ou ewe vif est trové,
E euwe de servour primes espuchez,
Car du peissoun la ne faudrez,
E si vous faudrez a cel estauncke
520   Ou le eauwe est adés coraunt,
Alez dounc saunz delai
Ou espleiteromes tut dreit au lay,
Car c'est eauwe en butemay.
524   La coveint pescher de nace
Ou petite rei ne trove grace.

That some take enough to get drunk on the spot.
Ale does wonders and marvels! It makes one candle into two
    candles![199]
Drunkenness makes a layman a clerk, it makes an unknown a
    man of mark,   504
It makes a strong man crawl, it makes a hoarse man shout aloud,
It makes a fool's face red without any vermilion;
After which they say, by George, he's had too much of the fat of
    the barley.
Here the author rests, because he wants to speak of something
    else.   512

Now the French for fishing in a pond or pool:

If you want to know how to fish in a fishpond
(It is properly called a *vivere* because it has living water in it)[200]
First drain off water from the reservoir,[201] because you won't lack
    fish there.
If you lack them in the pool[202] where water is always running,   520
Go without delay[203] and we'll hurry to the lake[204]
Because there's water in the marshlands.[205]
Where a little net is no use you must fish with a seine.

199. Manuscript T adds the marginal explanation in French *par yveresse*: it is 'by
    drunkenness' that one candle turns into two candles.
200. I.e., flowing water. Etymologically Walter is wrong: it is so called (Latin
    vivarium, French *vivier*) because live fish are kept in it. On this passage see
    Sayers 2008b.
201. Anglo-Norman *servour*. Since there is no gloss the word had perhaps already
    been borrowed into English (see *OED* 'server 2. a').
202. Anglo-Norman *estauncke* (French *étang*); English gloss *pool*. The loanword
    stank (see *OED* 'stank n.') was known in English by about 1300.
203. Anglo-Norman *delai*; English gloss *abiding*. The loanword *delay* (see *OED*
    'delay n.') was known in English by about 1275.
204. Anglo-Norman *lay* (a form of the familiar word *lac*); English gloss *grete
    pol*.
205. Anglo-Norman *butemay*; English gloss *muire* (see *OED* 'mire n.¹').

Il i ad nace e crivere ausi,
Commune fraunceis a chescuni.
528   La nace est menuement overez,
Mes plus large partuz assez
Ad le crivere, pur quei le di,
Car autre difference n'ad ici.
532   Mes returnoms a la matire
Ki de pescher vous voille dire.
Legurget de nace revercez,
L'ordure leins engettez.
536   Crapaude e lezart ne esparniez,
Serpent e colure ausi tuez;
Gravele e cailloun eruez,
E lymaçoun ausint destruez.
540   Si du pesschun i trovez,
Par les vemberges le pernez.
Ci il seit mulewel de mer,
Overer le devez e espander.
544   Le no tantost en oustez,
Bouwele e eschine ensi le frez.
Si returnez ver mesoun
Du gardin par cele crevessoun
548   Tant cum venés au vert terail
Ou le pastour est ou le aumail,
Puis par çoe bois in cel umbrail
Passerez desouz le hourail.
552   Mes dounc servent atant des peres
Ki sunt appelez passueres

There's sieve[206] and riddle, French names for both:
The sieve has smaller openings; much larger holes has the riddle,   528
Which is why I mention it: there's no other difference.
Let's return to the topic of fishing about which I wanted to tell
    you.
Turn back the neck[207] of the seine, throw out the dirt:[208]
Don't spare toad or newt;[209] kill adder[210] and grass-snake[211] too.   536
Take out grit and flint; also destroy snails.
If you find fish there, take them by the gills!
If they are codlings[212] you must open them and spread them;
Take out the sound,[213] guts, spine and bones.   544
Now return to the house by this gap in the garden wall,[214]
And when you come to that green balk[215] where the shepherd is
    with his animals,
Then through that wood in the shade go under the forest edge[216] –
But useful for this are the stones called stepping-stones   552

---

206. The digression is relevant because Anglo-Norman *nace* is used for both seine and sieve. Lines 526–533 are not in manuscript T.
207. English gloss *bothem*, i.e. 'bottom'.
208. English gloss *fulthe* (see *OED* 'filth n. 2. b.').
209. Anglo-Norman *lezart*, French *lézard*, the name of numerous Continental species, but if Walter is writing about England he must mean a newt; English gloss *hevete* (see *OED* 'eft n.¹'; newt').
210. Anglo-Norman *serpent*, as in French, the name of several Continental species, but if Walter is writing about England he must mean 'adder', *Vipera berus*. The English gloss is *neddre*, which, like *serpent*, was potentially a general term (see *OED* 'adder 2 1.') but must also mean 'adder' here.
211. See note at line 274.
212. Anglo-Norman *muluel, mulewel*, later borrowed into English (see *OED* 'mulvel; morhwell'); English gloss *keeling* (see *OED* 'keeling; codling'). Lines 542–545 are not in manuscript T.
213. Or swimming-bladder (*OED* 'sound n.¹ 2.').
214. Anglo-Norman *crevessoun*, introduced for the sake of the rhyme with *mesoun* 'house'.
215. An unploughed grassy strip (*OED* 'balk n.¹ II. 3.').
216. Anglo-Norman *hourail, uraille*; English glosses *wode hevese* (i.e. 'wood eaves') and *lindes* (see examples of 'under the lind' in *OED* 'lind 1., 2.').

Pur passer secke lé russeles
Ki sunt si clers e si beles.
556 Il i ad ourail par .h. escrit,
Orail ausi saunz .h. est dist.
Desouz le hourail se kevere laroun,
E par le orail oit meint hom.
560 Mes einz ki passez plus avaunt,
De terail vous ert plus disaunt,
Pur ceo qu'il ad plus de sens.
Dunt tel i ad il difference.
564 Il ad tenoun e terail,
E tenailles ki n'est merveille.
Li tenoun tent li cotyver,
E par le terail passe meinte ber,
568 Mes tenailles servent des carbuns
En yver quant au fu seoms,
E au fevre servent de custume
Quant du martel fert sur l'enclume.

Ore pur beau temps e pur tempeste

572 Ore pleut, ore geele;
Ore remet, ore regele.
Pur la gele avez vous glace
E par la glace avez vous vereglace,
576 E si n'est pas bon trop hastere
Sur vereglace pur vereglacere.
E geele e pluwe deguttaunt
Fount le chemin trop lidaunt.
580 Ore negge, ore cymeie.
Le cyme enpire nostre veie.
La bouche me entre un aumfe de neif.
Ja quident qi jeo euse grant seif.
584 Nos averoms grisil puis q'il grele,
Assez trop non pas trop grele.

To stay dry when crossing those clear and beautiful streams
There is *hourail* 'forest edge' with an *h* and *orail* 'ear' without the *h*;

A thief hides in the forest edge, while most people hear through
    their ears.
While you walk on, I have more to say about the green balk: 560
The word has several meanings, and this is how they differ.
There is crossbar and balk and tongs: no surprise there;
The ploughman holds the crossbar,[217] many a man crosses the balk,[218]
My tongs hold the coals in winter when we sit by the fire;   568
Tongs serve the blacksmith's turn when he hits the anvil with his
    hammer.

Now in good weather and in storm:

Now it rains, now it freezes, now it thaws, now it re-freezes.
When it freezes you have ice and with ice you have black ice;
It's not good to hurry too much or you'll slip on the black ice,[219]   576
And dripping ice and rain make the road too slippery.[220]
Now it snows, now it sleets,[221] and sleet worsens our path.
A snowflake goes into my mouth – it must have thought I was
    thirsty.
We'll have hail because it's hailing very heavily and not very   584
    small.[222]

217. Anglo-Norman *tenoun*; English gloss *handel*, perhaps imprecise. See line 918, where *handel* glosses *manual* and *stulte* glosses *tenoun*.
218. Perhaps, as suggested to me by William Sayers, this alludes to death and burial, 'passing over'. Lines 556–571 are not in manuscript T.
219. Cognates in Anglo-Norman: *vereglace* 'black ice' (literally glass-ice); *vereglacer* 'to slip'. English glosses for the noun are *ysikel* (*OED* 'icicle') and *slidernes* (*OED* 'slidderness' slipperiness), both inaccurate; perhaps there was no precise Middle English term for 'black ice'?
220. English gloss *szlidinde*, i.e. 'sliding'.
221. Anglo-Norman *cemeier*, a word ideally suited to England and not found in French sources.
222. Anglo-Norman *grisil* 'hail n.', *grele* 'it hails' (cognates) followed by the homonym *grele* 'small'.

Jeo oy toner; veir il tonne,
Dunt la cerveise empire en .tonne
588   Ore me suffrez, mon pee tonne.
Nul de vous mot ne sonne!
Freid est dil yver l'orer.
Un devinail voil demustrer.
592   En yver quant l'orere chaunge
Une verge i crest estrange.
Verge qui est saunz verdour
Sauns foil crest e saunz flour.
596   Quant vendra le chaut esté
La verge ne ert ja moustré.[5]
En yver quant l'orere chaunge
E le tens devient estraunge
600   Qi a meint hom fet fort endurer,
Pur le destreit del yver
Dunt avez la mein si estomie
Ki pur le freit ne purrez mie
604   Dé deis fere la capinole,
Meus vodroie suz plume mole
Seer prés du fu ki a la carole,

---

5.   T gives the explanation: *Red this redeles wat may be:* Ceo est un esclarzil, En engleys un *hyysikil.*

I hear thunder; it's really thundering, which makes beer spoil[223]
    in the tun.
Now wait, my foot's gone to sleep,[224] so don't anyone make a noise!
The winter wind is cold, and I'll tell you a riddle:
In winter when the wind changes a strange branch grows,   592
A branch without greenery grows without leaf or flower;
When hot summer comes the branch will no longer be seen.[225]
Read this riddle what it may be!
It's an *esclarcil*, in English an icicle.[226]
In winter when the wind changes and the weather grows unfriendly
And makes many men suffer, in the depth of winter   600
From which your hand is cumbered[227] so that you are unable
To clench your fist,[228]
I prefer to sit on soft feathers near the fire rather than at the
    dancing

223. One might say 'turn', but this near-homonym would not have occurred to Walter: 'turn' was apparently not used in this sense in English before the 16th century (*OED* 'turn v. 46. b.'). It is a commonplace that thundery weather causes wine and beer to turn sour in the cask.

224. Three cognates, Anglo-Norman *toner* 'thunder n.', *toune* 'it thunders' and *toune* 'go numb, go to sleep', apparently a back-formation from *estouner* (French *étonner*). The latter appears in various forms in English: *astone*, *astun*, *stony* v., *stoyne* and (possibly) *stun*. Alongside these is the homonym *toune* 'tun, cask'.

225. There is a continuing play on the words *verge* 'branch' and *vert* 'green'.

226. The line in English, and the couplet giving the answer to the riddle, occur only in manuscript T. The riddle also occurs in a fragmentary Cambridge manuscript not connected with Walter's writings (see Braunholtz 1921). This is another icicle error (compare note 219): *esclarcil*, though it sounds like the English word, is not the French for an icicle.

227. English gloss *comeled* (see *OED* 'cumble v., cumber v.') is said to mean 'numbed with cold' and to derive from Anglo-Norman *combler* 'overload' (< Latin *cumulare*), but Walter does not use that word here. Compare also Old French *combre* 'bent over, hollowed'.

228. Anglo-Norman *faire la capinole* 'make a clenched fist'. English glosses +*hant motile*, *crowke* (cf. *OED* 'crouch v., crouk', though they are not used of the hand), *kattes clawe* (a nice expression which is not in *OED* in this sense). Lines 598–604 are not in manuscript T.

Chapeu vestu de blauverole,
608 Ou de quiller primerole
Pur fere chapeus a clers d'escole,
Ki par bost qui ne vaut frivole
E par knyvet ou virole
612 Savent attrere femme fole.
Dunc teus ki sunt de tel escole
Vaudroient plus en la jayhole
Ki jeuene femme en oriole,
616 Car quer de femme est si mole,
Esquier ou clerke quant l'acole,
Ki sovent a bref parole
Femme fole le recole.
620 Ore pleut a Deu qe tels foles
Ussent faces pleins de veroles,
E teus ribaus les rugeroles.
Si lerreint dunc les braceroles

Wearing a wreath of cornflowers, or gathering primroses   608
To make garlands for schoolmen who, with boasting[229] that's not
    worth a fennel-stalk,[230]
With blade or virl[231] know how to attract a silly woman[232] –
And all who are of that school are better in jail
Than a young woman in her chamber,
For the heart of woman is so soft that when a squire or scholar   616
    embraces[233] her
Often after a brief word the foolish woman returns the
    embrace.[234]
Please God such women should have faces covered with pox,
And such men with measles,[235] so that they will give up their
    cuddles,[236]

229. Anglo-Norman *bost*, a borrowing from English not otherwise recorded (Rothwell 2009, p. 27 note 8).

230. English gloss *kex* as at line 465 above. A close English equivalent to *ne vaut frenole* would be 'not worth a rush', a phrase first recorded in 1362 (see *OED* 'rush n. 2. a. (b)').

231. The metal band around the haft of a knife. The English names (*OED* 'ferrule, verrel, virole, virl') are all loanwords from Anglo-Norman *verole*. Walter returns to this word below. As Sayers suggests to me, 'with blade or virl' equates to 'by hook or crook'.

232. Anglo-Norman *femme fole*. There is no gloss; perhaps the English *fool* (borrowed from Anglo-Norman) was already used as an adjective in the same sense. Note e. g. *fole maydens* in the story of the wise and foolish virgins (*Mirour of Saluacioun* [*c.* 1450] line 271).

233. English gloss *beclippe* (see *OED* 'beclip v.¹').

234. Last of a series of 16 rhymes in -*ole*, from *capinole* 'clenched fist' to *recole* 'return the embrace'. Now follow 6 rhymes in -*oles*.

235. English gloss *maselinges* (see *OED* 'measlings'). On this passage see Sayers 2010d.

236. English glosses *clipping*, *halsing* (the latter is commonly combined in Middle English in the censorious phrase *halsing and kissing*). The English verb *halse* (*OED* 'halse v.²') derives from *halse* 'neck' just as Anglo-Norman *acoler* and *recoler* derive from *col* 'neck'; it may be a loan-translation.

624 E les foles les karoles,
   E eschureint les blaces foles.
   Mes pur aprendre ces innocens,
   Des viroles dirrai plus dé sens.
628 Il i ad virole e verole
   Ki sunt de diverse escole.
   La virole la maunche garde
   De cotel li mau musard,
632 Mes la verole la face enpire
   Ne seit ja de si grant sire,
   Mes c'est une varole pure
   Ki de cholet crest par nature.
636 Un verme ki vert est coluré.
   En Fraunce est varole nomé.

Ore le fraunceis des flurs e des fruz du verger

   Le jour devient trop beaus e cler.
   Alom dedure ou banoer
640 Au verget ou sunt les fluirs
   Dunt en issent les duz odurs,
   Herbes ausi pur medicine,
   Dunt les noms ci vous divine.
644 Fluir de rose e fluir de lys.
   Liz vaut pur roingne, rose pur pis.

And the foolish women their dancing, and keep away from bad 624
    places.[237]
But to teach innocent children I'll say more of the meanings of
    virole.
There is virl and variola and they belong to different schools:
The virl guards the handle of a careless man's knife
But variola spoils a man's face however great he is, 632
While a real *varole* grows naturally on a cabbage leaf,
Because in France a green caterpillar is called a *varole*.[238]

Now the French of orchard flowers and fruits:

The day has turned very fine and bright. Let's go and have fun:
    let's play
In the orchard, where there are flowers that give off sweet scents, 640
Herbs useful in medicine, too, and I shall now tell you their names.
Rose flower,[239] yellow flag:[240] flag is good for gripes, rose for the
    chest.

237. Last of a series of 6 rhymes (varying only by the final –s from the previous
    series), the first and last identical: *foles* 'foolish women'.
238. Anglo-Norman *verole* 'variola, smallpox', *virole* 'virl, ferrule' (see above), *varole*
    'cabbage-white caterpillar, *Pieris rapae*'. English glosses for *varole*: +*wratte*,
    wortworm. The English *virl* and its more familiar synonym *ferrule* both derive
    from the Anglo-Norman. Lines 626–637 are not in manuscript T.
239. *Rosa spp.*, Anglo-Norman *fluir de rose*. The English was also *rose* (borrowed
    by Old English and other Germanic languages from Latin); hence there is
    no gloss.
        Walter's French phraseology leads him to specify the flower in these two
    cases. Rose hip (rather than flower) was used to treat chest ailments, according
    to *Old English Herbarium* ch. 170, de Vriend 1984, pp. 214–215.
240. *Iris pseudacorus*, Anglo-Norman *fluir de lys*, borrowed into English by about
    this time (see *OED* 'fleur-de-lis') and replacing the older English name
    gladdon; hence there is no gloss. The later term *yellow flag* (apparently
    borrowed from Dutch) began to replace fleur-de-lis in the 16th century.
        The bulb of gladdon, i.e. yellow flag, was used for pain in the bladder
    and spleen, the flower for heartburn and intestinal pain, according to *Old
    English Herbarium* ch. 80, de Vriend 1984, pp. 120–121.

Ausi i crest la fluir de surcye,
Ki a les eus fet grant aye.

648   Primerole e prineveir
Qui tost se mustrent en tens de veir.
Here du bois e here terrestre
En ceo boys deivent crestre.

652   Ci ert assez de plauntayne
E bugle ausi, herbe saine.
Cerlaunge ki sovent crest en crevez,
Une herbe qe severouse redirez,

Also marigold grows there and is not jealous of the eyebrows;[241]
The oil taken from marigolds finds great use under the brows.   648
Primrose[242] and cowslip,[243] which show early in spring,
Wood ivy[244] and ale-hoof[245] are sure to grow in this wood;
There will be plantain[246] enough and also bugle,[247] a healthy herb;
Hart's-tongue[248] which often grows in crevices,[249] a herb that
    cures acne;[250]

241. Essentially a play on homonyms: eyebrow is Anglo-Norman *sourcil*; marigold, *Calendula officinalis*, is Anglo-Norman *fluir de surcye*. The English glosses for marigold are *gold-flower, solsecle*: the latter is borrowed from old French *solsecle*, cognate with the Anglo-Norman; both derive from Latin *solsequium* (*ML* no. 8078). The English translation in *Femina* supplies a third English gloss, *flour of the rode* (see *OED* 'rud v.²'; rodewort').

    There is something to the juxtaposition beyond homonymy: *solsequia* pounded in oil could be used to treat swellings such as styes. See for example *Old English Herbarium* ch. 76, de Vriend 1984, pp. 116–117, though I note that de Vriend identifies the *solosece* and *solsequia* of this text with deadly nightshade or garden nightshade.

242. *Primula vulgaris*, Anglo-Norman *primerole*. The word was borrowed into English about this time (later supplanted by *primrose*; see *OED* 'primerole, primrose n.'); hence there is no gloss.

243. *Primula veris*, Anglo-Norman *prineveir*; English gloss *kousloppe*.

244. *Hedera helix*, Anglo-Norman *here du bois*; English gloss *hyvy tre* 'ivy tree'.

245. *Glechoma hederacea*, Anglo-Norman *here terrestre* (cf. modern French *lierre terrestre*). English gloss *heyhove* (see *OED* 'ground-ivy 1. a, hayhove, ale-hoof').

246. *Plantago major*, Anglo-Norman *plauntayne*; English gloss *weibrede* (see *OED* 'waybread').

247. *Ajuga reptans*, Anglo-Norman *bugle*. In English *bugle* (see *OED* 'bugle n.²'), borrowed from Anglo-Norman, was already replacing the alternative English name *wood-brown*; hence manuscript G has no English gloss. The gloss in manuscript T is *oxtongue*, a translation for *buglosse* (*Anchusa arvensis*) not *bugle*. The same confusion occurs in other early texts.

248. *Scolopendrium vulgare*. Anglo-Norman *cerlange*, which, to judge by its structure, is not independent of English *hart's-tongue*. Elsewhere, and in later French, the form is *langue de cerf*. English gloss *hertetonge*.

249. English gloss *chine* (see *OED* 'chine n.¹ 2.').

250. As suggested in *AND*. Anglo-Norman *severouse*, a word of unknown meaning.

656   E ausi troverez plenté des navez,
      Consoude la blanche fluir
      E mercurial de grant valour.
      Pur sause vaut la surele,
660   Pur home teignous la parele.
      Parele i ad, parele e pareaus.
      De tote manere des oyseaus
      Une couple ad de mal e femel;
664   C'est un parel, non pas parele.
      E ausi sunt pareaus nomez
      Puis ki ensemble sunt niez.
      Uncore as flures me voil aler
668   Ki ne fest mie a ublier,
      Car hermoise vous troverez
      E plantayne si la semmez.
      E si vous trovez au verger
672   Ameroke e gletoner
      Les arassez de une besagu
      E plauntez cholet en lur liu.

Also you'll find plenty of bryony,[251]   656
The white flower of daisy[252] and the very valuable mercury;[253]
Sorrel[254] is good for sauce, red dock[255] helps with scab
There's *parele, parel* and *pareau*; of every kind of bird
There's a couple, male and female: *parel* (alike), not *parele* (red dock), 664
But also *pareaus* (pairs) because they nest together).[256]
I want to go back to the flowers again; they are not to be forgotten
Because you'll find mugwort[257] there, and plantain if you sow it;
And if you find mayweed[258] and burdock[259] growing there   672
Get them out with a mattock[260] and plant cabbage-sprouts[261] in
    their place.

---

251. Walter's text has *navet* and the English gloss in manuscript T is *of nepes*. Since turnips are not wild flowers of wood or orchard, pace Rothwell 2009, Walter cannot mean turnips: evidently he means bryony, *Bryonia dioica*. Compare the glossary *Alphita* (*c.* 1450) cited by *OED* s.v. 'nep n.[2] wild nep': *Vitis alba, brionia idem. gall. navet, angl. wildnep*. See also *OED* 'nip n. 2'.

252. *Bellis perennis*, Anglo-Norman *consoude*; English glosses *dayseie, dayes hye*.

253. *Mercurialis spp.*, Anglo-Norman *mercurial*. English glosses *smerdocke, smerwort*.

254. *Rumex acetosa*, Anglo-Norman *surele*. English gloss *surdoke* (see *OED* 'sour dock').

255. *Rumex sanguineus*. English glosses +*roddok, reddokke* (see *OED* 'dock n.[1] 1. b. red dock').

256. A play on words which works in Anglo-Norman but not in English: *pareau* 'pair'; *parele* 'red dock'; *parel* 'alike'. Lines 661–670 are not in manuscript T.

257. *Artemisia vulgaris*, Anglo-Norman *hermoise*. English gloss *mogwede* (see *OED* 'mugweed a.').

258. *Anthemis cotula*, stinking chamomile. Anglo-Norman *ameroke*, which survives in modern Norman *amuerok*; later French *maroute*. English gloss *maythe* (see *OED* 'maythe, maidweed, mayweed').

259. *Arctium lappa*, Anglo-Norman *gletoner*; English gloss *clote* (see *OED* 'clete, clite, clithe, clote').

260. English gloss *tuybil* (see *OED* 'twibill, tubbal').

261. Anglo-Norman *cholet* 'spring cabbage shoots', perhaps already familiar in English since there is no gloss. It is now a dialect word (cf. *OED* 'collard'): *collards* (Essex, southern United States and elsewhere), *collets* (Oxfordshire), *colluts* (Berkshire).

Ore le fraunceis des arbres du verger

En ceo verger des arbres creissent.
676   Par charge des fruiz lé uns abesent.
Pomer, perere e cereiser,
Freine, genest e pruner,
Ceneiller qe ceneilles porte,
680   E le fouder qe lé foudeines aporte;
Englenter ki lespeperonges comporte,
Crekere ki les crekes forporte.
Ly alier port les alies,
684   Dunt Alianore en auncieneries
Le noun reçust de un rey
Ki out aliez en or devaunt sei.
Tut ausi crest li coingner.
688   Sovent le veit hom au verger.
Mes si ad diverseté grant
Ki ne sevent mie aquaunt.

Now the French of orchard trees:

Trees are growing in the orchard, some bowed down by their load
    of fruit:
Apple tree,[262] pear tree [263] and cherry tree,[264] ash,[265] broom [266] and
    plum tree,[267]
Hawthorn bearing haws [268] and blackthorn bringing sloes,[269]   680
Dog-rose clothed in rose-hips,[270] bullace-tree putting forth
    bullaces,[271]
And service-tree bearing golden *alies*,[272] from which Eleanor in
    times of old
Received her name, because the king had *alies en or* before him.[273]
And in this orchard there will also be a dry quince-tree [274]
    standing.   688
There's some variation here, and people don't know the range of
    it:

262. Anglo-Norman *pomer*; English gloss *appiltre* (*OED* 'apple-tree').
263. Anglo-Norman *perer*; English gloss *peretre* (*OED* 'pear-tree').
264. Anglo-Norman *cereiser*; English gloss *chiritre* (*OED* 'cherry-tree').
265. Anglo-Norman *freine*; English gloss *haish* (*OED* 'ash n.¹').
266. Anglo-Norman *genest*; English gloss *brom* (*OED* 'broom n.').
267. Anglo-Norman *pruner*; English gloss *plontre* (*OED* 'plum-tree').
268. Anglo-Norman *ceneiller, ceneilles*; English gloss *hawethen, hawes* (*OED* 'hawthorn, haw n.²').
269. Anglo-Norman *fouder, foudeines* according to Walter; the more expected term *prunele* is offered by *St John's E.17* (Acker 1993); English gloss *slothorne, slos* (*OED* 'sloe-thorn, sloe').
270. *Rosa canina*, Anglo-Norman *englenter, peperonges*; English gloss *brere, hepes* (*OED* 'brier n.¹, hip n.²').
271. Anglo-Norman *crekere, crekes*; English gloss *bolastre, bolas* (*OED* 'bullester, bullace'). *Creker* for a bullace-tree is rare in Anglo-Norman: for another example see the *Nominale* (Skeat 1906) as cited by *OED* s.v. 'plum-tree'.
272. *Sorbus domestica* or *S. aria*. Anglo-Norman *alier, alies*; English glosses *cirnetre* and *cirves* (see *OED* 'service-tree, service n.²').
273. 'Golden service-berries'. Eleanor of Aquitaine, the earliest confirmed bearer of this name, was born about 120 years before Walter wrote. The true derivation of *Aliénor* is uncertain, but this is not it.
274. Anglo-Norman *coingner*; English gloss *quincetre*.

Li seignur fet sun cneif coingner
692 En ces ceps pur chastier.
Pernez un coing, si batés le secke coingner
E coupez du coinun coigner.
E coingner est il ensement
696 Ki fet la moneie del argent.
Des autres arbres i sunt ausi.
Pur meuz aprendre chescuni,
Buit i ad, paumere e arable
700 Ki n'est suffert en tere arable.
Mes a verger crest la houce,
Ki de nint ne vaut pur houce,
E le sueau i crest ausi,
704 Commune fust a chescuni.
Sauz i crest e cheine e if;
De ceo fraunceis n'ad guers d'estrif,

The lord has his knave confined in the stocks to punish him;
Take the poleaxe, chop down the quince-tree, cut a wedge with
    the axe
And send it to the coiner[275] who makes the money.   696
There are still other trees: if you want to learn them all
There's box,[276] palm tree,[277] maple (not allowed to grow in
    farmland),[278]
But in the orchard holly grows, useless for a tabard,[279]
And the elder grows there too, well known to everybody,[280]   704
Willow[281] grows there, oak[282] and yew,[283] and there's no trouble
    about the French

275. End of a series of cognates and homonyms: Anglo-Norman *coingner* 'quince tree; to confine'; *coigner* 'wedge'; *coing* 'quince'; *coin* 'axe, poleaxe'. The last in the series, *coingner* 'coiner, moneyer', is familiar in English but not otherwise known in Anglo-Norman or French (Rothwell 2009, p. 31 note 15).

276. *Buxus sempervirens*, Anglo-Norman *buit*; English gloss *box*.

277. Anglo-Norman *paumere*; English gloss *palmetre*. There's no surprise here. Local trees were substituted in religious ritual for the palm that does not grow in northern Europe, and were locally called 'palm tree'; most often perhaps willow and yew, but Walter names both of these below; also hazel, which is not otherwise mentioned in this passage.

278. *Acer campestre*, Anglo-Norman *arable*; English gloss *mapil* (*OED* 'maple').

279. Homonyms, *houce* 'holly' and *houce* (variant of *huce*) 'tabard'. *Ilex aquifolium*, English gloss *holintre* (see *OED* 'holly').

280. *Sambucus nigra*, Anglo-Norman *sueau*; English gloss *helren* (see *OED* 'elder n.').

281. *Salix spp.*, Anglo-Norman *sauz*; English gloss *wilwe* (see *OED* 'willow n.').

282. *Quercus spp.*, Anglo-Norman *cheine*; English gloss *hoke* (*OED* 'oak').

283. *Taxus baccata*, Anglo-Norman *if*; English gloss *iv* (see *OED* 'yew'; forms resembling Walter's are found in other early medieval texts). Not 'ivy' as suggested by Rothwell 2009, p. 32 note 6.

Car le langage est ben commune
708   E de clerck e de clerjoune.
Du sueth l'em fet sueaus,
Un manger bon e beaus.

Ore le fraunceis des oyseaus dé bois

Quant du verger avom le chois,
712   Aloms ore juer a boys
Ou la russinole, *the nichtingale,*
Meuz chaunte ki houswan en sale.
E meuz chaunte mauviz en busson
716   Ki ne fet chauf sorriz en meisoun.
En branche set le menue merle.
En mareis demert la herle.

Because this vocabulary is well known to scholar and student
(From elder is made *sueaus*,[284] a good and pleasant food).

Now the French of birds of the forest:

From the orchard I'm going straight on to the wood   712
Where the nightingale[285] sings better than a tawny owl[286] in a
 hall,
As a song-thrush[287] sings better in a bush than a bat does in a
 house.
The little blackbird[288] sits on a branch; the sheldrake[289] lives in
 the marsh.

284. The Anglo-Norman name for the dishes flavoured with elderflower called
    suade, suth in Middle English (there is no confusion with suet, as suggested by
    Rothwell 2009, p. 32 note 7). What looks like an English gloss, in manuscript
    T, turns out to be a suggested recipe: *wit mylk*. More helpful recipes, requiring
    almond milk, are found in *Diversa Cibaria* and *Diversa Servicia* (Hieatt and
    Butler 1985), and in Anglo-Norman in BL Royal 12.C.xii: *Let d'alemaunz,
    amydon ou la lyure des flurs de swade; les flurs deyvent estre plumees e mys
    en gyngyvre grant plenté; les flurs de swade plaunté desuis; colour, blanc.*
    'Elder-flower pottage. Almond milk, with wheat starch and elder flowers as
    thickeners; the flowers should be stripped from the stems and rolled in plenty
    of ginger; elder flowers set on top; the colour, white' (text and translation
    from Hieatt and Jones 1986, pp. 867, 878). A more complex dish called *suet
    blanc* included chicken or fish: see the recipe in *Coment l'en deit fere viande e
    claree* (Hieatt and Jones 1986, pp. 865, 876). For more on medieval elderflower
    dishes such as sambocade see Hieatt 1988, p. 15.
285. *Luscinia megarhynchos*. The verse gives both Anglo-Norman and English: *la
    russinole, the nichtingale.*
286. *Strix aluco*. English gloss *houle*, less specific than the Anglo-Norman *huan* (for
    which Walter's text has *houswan*); English is poorer than French in names
    for owls.
287. *Turdus philomelos*, Anglo-Norman *mauviz*; English gloss *throstel* (see *OED*
    'throstle').
288. *Turdus merula*, Anglo-Norman *merle*; English gloss *osel* (see *OED* 'ouzel 1.
    a.').
289. *Tadorna tadorna*. Anglo-Norman *herle*; English gloss *sheldedrake.*

Uncore il ad ausi filaundre
720   E le oysel ki ad noun chalaundre.[6]
Au four meint le salemaundre.
Suffrez le pesschon espaundre.
Mes il i ad espandre e espaundre,
724   Espendre ensement e pandre.
Cil espandi conceil d'amy
Ki li deskevre a nuly,
E li enfez de gré espaunde
728   Hors de sa quele sa viande.
E des eylés paunde peschoun
Quant vif en rei le prent hom.

6.   For 719–720 T has: Regardez cy Alysaundre Un herbe apelé alysaundre. Regardez cy la filaundre *(gosesomer)*. Escoutez cum chaunte la chalaundre *(wodelarke)*.

See here, Alexander, a herb called alexanders![290]
Look at the starling[291] and listen to the woodlark's[292] song;   720
The salamander[293] is in the oven; let the fish spawn![294]
But there's spread and shed and also spell and flap:[295]
One spreads a friend's opinion if one tells it to anyone;
The child likes to shed or spill his food from his dish;   728
Fish flap[296] their fins when a man takes them live in a net;

290. *Smyrnium olusatrum*. Anglo-Norman *alysaundre*, cognate with English *alexanders* (both apparently borrowed from the Latin name *petroselinum alexandrinum*); hence there is no gloss.

291. *Sturnus vulgaris*. Anglo-Norman *filaundre*. English gloss *stare* (see *OED* 'stare n.¹') in manuscript G; in manuscript T the gloss is *gossamer*.

292. *Lullula arborea*. Anglo-Norman *chalaundre* (cognate with Italian *calandra*, which is properly the name of the calandra lark, *Melanocorypha calandra*, a species unknown in France and England). These two couplets are translated from manuscript T, adding one couplet to the total.

293. Anglo-Norman *salemaundre* 'salamander', a yellow and black lizard-like creature with the reputation of being able to withstand fire. English gloss *criket*, completely inaccurate but found elsewhere too; compare Langland, *Piers Plowman* 'Fissch to lyue in the flode and in the fire the crykat'; John of Trevisa, *Bartholomaeus Anglicus de proprietatibus rerum* 'The crekette hyght salamandra: for thys beest quencheth fyre and lyueth in brennynge fyre' (both cited by *OED*). Thus Walter's 'salamander in the oven' led to Milton's 'cricket on the hearth'.

294. *Espaundre* 'spawn': English gloss *scheden his rowe* 'shed its roe'. End of a series of rhymes that began and ended with nonsense: *alysaundre* (twice), *filaundre*, *chalaundre*, *salemaundre*, *espaundre*.

295. Three near-homonyms in Anglo-Norman: *espandre* 'spread, shed'; *pandre* 'flap'; *espaudre* 'spell'. The last (in the slightly older form *espeldre*) had already been borrowed into Middle English as *spelder* (see *OED* 'spelder') with the precise meaning specified by Walter here, 'to spell out, read phonetically'. Later a Middle French form of the same word, *espeler*, was borrowed again into English as *spell* (see *OED* 'spell v.²'). *Espeldre/espeler* was a Germanic loanword in French, and the Germanic word already existed in Old English with a slightly different meaning (see *OED* 'spell v.1').

This line marks the end of a series of six rhymes. The bird-names *filaundre* and *chalaundre* led on via *salamaundre* to 'spawn' and its homonyms.

296. English gloss *flakerers* (see *OED* 'flack v., flacker v.'). Lines 723–750 are not in manuscript T.

Mes espaudere est la quarte parole,
732 E ceo funt lé clerjouns d'escole,
Car espeau naturément
Ki les lettres ensemble prent.
Eyles e eeles sunt divers,
736 Descordaunt dient ces clers.
Des eiles neent ces peschons,
Des eeles volent ces moschouns.
Ausi ad il naer e noer e nager
740 Dunt la resoun fest a saver.
En mer nee li peschoun,
E en mer noe meinte prodom.
Mes des virouns deivent nager
744 En bateles li mariner.
Mes en yver veoms negger
E les aumfes avaler.
Ore a oyseaus rediroms
748 Ou plus aprendre i purroms.
En chaumbre e aillurs ausi
Depeint home ceste oysel asci.
Mes veez ou tapist un ascie.
752 Fraunceis veut ke l'em si die.
Plus avaunt ore venés
E ceo ki verrez entendés,
Car il i ad vereder e verder,
756 L'un oysel, l'autre forester;
Car par cy vole le vereuder
Et par la voit li forester.
Ci vient volaunt un restel
760 E se trest ver cele tresel.

But the fourth word is spell, and this is what students do at
    school,
Because when you put letters together you spell words.
Fins and wings are different,[297] discordant as scholars say: 736
Fish swim with their fins, sparrows fly with their wings.
Now there's swim, drown and row,[298] and you must be able to tell
    them apart:
Fish swim in the sea, some good people drown in it,
Mariners[299] in boats have to row their oars;   744
But in winter, as we see, it snows and snowflakes fall.
Now we'll return to the birds, because we can learn more from
    them.
In a chamber – elsewhere too – people paint the bird called
    woodcock,[300]
But look where a woodcock hides: a Frenchman wants to hear   752
Because woodcock is the style of the citizens of York.[301]
Now come further on and see what you can see:
There's a robin and a verderer,[302] one a bird, the other a forester!
The robin flies this way because he sees the forester that way.
This way a wren[303] comes flying, and turns towards that stook of
    corn   760

297. Walter gives two spellings for what is the same Anglo-Norman word, *eele*,
    eyle, 'wing, fin'.
298. Anglo-Norman *naer* 'to swim', *noer* 'to drown', *nager* 'to row' (the last has
    come to mean 'swim' in modern French), a series of near-homonyms with
    similar meanings; a fourth comes to mind afterwards, *negger* 'to snow'.
299. English gloss *shipmen* (see *OED* 'shipman 1.'). Anglo-Norman *mariner* was
    borrowed into English at about this time.
300. *Scolopax rusticola*. Anglo-Norman *asci*; its other name *bekas* is used below by
    Walter with the meaning 'snipe'.
301. A joke whose point escapes me. Woodcocks are easily fooled; has the same
    been true of the citizens of York? Why does this interest a Frenchman? This
    passage is one couplet longer in manuscript T.
302. Near homonyms: Anglo-Norman *vereder* 'robin' (*Prunella modularis*; English
    gloss *roddocke*, see *OED* 'ruddock'), *verder* 'verderer, forester'.
303. *Troglodytes troglodytes*. Anglo-Norman *restel* (modern French *roitelet*); English
    gloss *wranne* (*OED* 'wren').

Car de asciés meuz vaut a restel
Vironer en un beau trescel,
Ki un beau treste de la viele
764 Ou nule note de frestele.
Uncore avez le musenge
Ki les haies u boys renge.
Deslacez, valet, toust ta renge,
768 Si renger volez le musenge.
Uncore i ad la palevole
E ausi la chardonerole.
E si ad des papilouns
772 Ki volunters seent en chardouns,
E en les runces ensement
Usent de seer naturelment.
E ceo ne fet pas li grissilour
776 Ki en curtillage ad sun sojour,
Ne li hirchoun nent lui pluis
Ki prent le poume qe chet jus,

Because the wren wants to fly around a good stook
More than a good saw on a fiddle[304] or any note on a flute.
Then you have the titmouse[305] ranging the hedges and woods:
Boy, undo your sword-belt if you want to chase[306] the titmouse.   768
Then there is the ladybird[307] and also the goldfinch,[308]
And there are butterflies that like to be on thistles
And by their nature often rest on brambles,[309] too,
But grasshoppers[310] don't: they live in gardens.   776
And the hedgehog[311] doesn't, who takes a windfall apple,

304. Play on words, especially in manuscript G: *trest* 'turns' and *beau trescel* 'good stook' reflected in *beau treste de la viele* 'good saw on a fiddle'. The rhyme words *restel* 'wren' and *trescel* 'stook' occur twice each.

305. *Parus sp.* Anglo-Norman *musenge* (modern French *mésange*); English gloss *titomoze*. The two words are cognates, believe it or not. *Titmouse* is a compound based on Old English *máse* 'titmouse'; *musenge* is borrowed from Frankish **meisinga* or Old Norse *meisingr*, cf. Old High German *meise* 'titmouse'.

306. Cognates: Anglo-Norman *renger* 'to range, to chase'; *renge* 'sword-belt', both deriving from Frankish **hring* 'ring'.

307. *Coccinella septempunctata* and others. Anglo-Norman *palevole*. English gloss in manuscript G *the rede fleye*; in another manuscript, *godyscou*; in manuscript T the very helpful *lite bode fle to wode*, a neater medieval version of the modern *ladybird, ladybird, fly away home*. These medieval terms, *palevole, red fly, God's cow* and *little body* are rarely found in other texts, but their meaning is not in doubt. The modern English names *lady-fly* and *lady-bird* are recorded only from the 18th century, preceded by *lady-cow* and *cow-lady* from the early 17th.

308. *Carduelis carduelis.* Anglo-Norman *chardonerole* for the sake of the rhyme (but preferably *chardonerel*); English gloss *golfinges*.

309. *Rubus fruticosus* and other species. Anglo-Norman *runce*; English gloss *brere*, the same term that is used above as a gloss for *englenter* 'dog-rose' (see note 270); it was at this period correctly used for brambles too. The equation of *rounce* and *brere* is confirmed by *St John's E.17* (Acker 1993).

310. Anglo-Norman *grissilour* (for the sake of the rhyme; preferably *grisilloun*). English gloss *grasshop*.

311. *Erinaceus europaeus.* Anglo-Norman *hirchoun*; English gloss also *hirchoun*. The word had indeed already been borrowed into English (see *OED* 'hercheon, irchin, urchin').

Ne mouches ne wibés ne funt mie,
780 Car il eiment plus la urtie.
Ausi ad il anede e plumjoun
Ki en vyvere unt lur mansioun.
En mores meinent les waneles.
784 En viles sunt les veneles.
En graunge usom la vaanne;
En quer de enviouse est le haane.
Ci vient volaunt un ouwe roser,
788 Un blaret ou li associer.
E meuz serroie de un blareth pu
Ke ne serroie du char de fru.
E pluis est ignele un arounde
792 Ki nul sygoun parmi le munde.

Nor do flies or gnats, which prefer nettles;[312]
Also there are ducks and dippers[313] whose home is in the
    fishpond.
Lapwings[314] and wagtails[315] do their chattering on the moors.
On moors live lapwings, in towns there are alleys,[316]   784
In the barn we use a winnowing-fan;[317] in the heart of a jealous
    woman is hatred.
Here comes flying a marsh-goose,[318] and a brent goose[319] beside
    him.
Better to eat a brent goose than the flesh of a rook;[320]
A swallow is swifter than any stork in the world.   792

312. *Urtica dioica.* Anglo-Norman *urtie*; English gloss *netle*. Lines 779–780 are
    not in manuscript T.

313. *Cinclus cinclus* and others. Anglo-Norman *plunjeon*; English gloss *dukere* (see
    OED 'ducker[1] 2.').

314. *Vanellus vanellus.* Anglo-Norman *vanele*; English gloss *wype*.

315. *Motacilla alba.* Anglo-Norman *pounzout*; English gloss *wanster* (see *OED*
    'washer n.[1] 4. a'). This couplet is added from manuscript T.

316. Near-homonyms: Anglo-Norman *vaneles* 'lapwings' and *veneles* 'alleys'.

317. Anglo-Norman *vaanne*; English gloss *fanne* (see *OED* 'fan n.[1] 1.'). The French
    and English are cognates, both deriving from Latin *vannus*. Later the Anglo-
    Norman form was borrowed directly into English (see *OED* 'van n.[1] 1.').
    Haane 'hatred' comes in for the sake of the rhyme.

318. *Anser cinereus*, greylag goose, the first domesticated species of geese, smaller
    than farmyard geese. Anglo-Norman *ouwe roser* and *houhe roser*, literally 'reed
    goose'; the modern French *oie rosière* is overlooked by most dictionaries, but
    see e.g. Roché 1999, p. 281. Acker 1993 adds the medieval Latin *auca rosera*.
    English gloss *wilde ges*. The Anglo-Norman names have possible English
    cognates, recorded later. See *OED* 'rat-goose; road-goose; roger 2. a.; rood
    goose'; also 'marsh II. 4. b. marsh-goose'. But *redlag* (cf. modern 'greylag'
    and the Scottish name *ridlaik*) is given as Middle English equivalent for *ouwe
    roser* in the glossary in *St John's E.17*: on the 'lag' element see Lockwood 1984,
    p. 74.

319. *Branta bernicla.* Anglo-Norman *blaret*. English glosses *brendgos* (see *OED*
    'brant n.; brent'), *belled gos*; in other texts glossed as *bernak* (see *OED*
    'barnacle n.²').

320. Anglo-Norman *fru* (elsewhere Latin *frugella* and *frigo*).

E severoundel a la cheverounde
Prent le meissoun e le arounde.
E li oisel ke ad noun bekas
796 Pres du river est pris a las.
Le chaunt de kokel est recous,
E si n'est guers delicious.
Poynt serreit si riotuse
800 Si sun chaunt fu graciouse.
E plus est oi en oriol
Ki la noise l'orkoil.

Ore le fraunceis des bestes du boys

En fraunceis plus avant me voise
804 Pur veer les estres du boyse.
Jeo vi vener un graunt tesschoun
Ki ad guerpi sa mansioun
Pur les fens du gupil
808 Ki l'ad mis en exil.

A sparrow-net[321] in the eaves catches sparrows and swallows.
The bird whose name is snipe[322] is caught with a noose[323] beside
the river.
The cuckoo's[324] song is loud and it's hardly a delicacy.
It wouldn't be so troublesome[325] if its song was graceful,   800
And it's heard more often in ladies' chambers than the song of the
oriole.[326]

Now the French of animals of the forest:

Let me go further in French and look at the creatures of the forest.
I see a big badger[327] coming this way: he has given up his house
To the droppings[328] of the fox[329] who has sent him into exile.   808

---

321. Anglo-Norman *severoundel*, derived from *cheverounde* 'eaves'. English gloss
sparou nett (see *OED* 'sparrow 4. a. sparrow-net', cited from 1621).

322. *Gallinago spp.* Anglo-Norman *bekas*, which can also mean 'woodcock', cf.
modern French *bécasse*, but Walter has used the word *asci* for 'woodcock'
above. *St John's E.17* confirms the equation of *bekaz* and *snype* (Acker 1993).
English glosses *snype*, *snyte* (see *OED* 'snipe n.; snite n.¹').

323. Anglo-Norman *las*, which had already been borrowed into English (see *OED*
'lace n.'); but the English gloss here is *streing*.

324. *Cuculus canorus*. Anglo-Norman *kokel*, which had already been borrowed
into English or had influenced the Old English *géac*; hence the English gloss
kochou. *St John's E.17* (Acker 1993) offers *cuccuke*; other texts give *cuckow*
etc.

325. Anglo-Norman *riotous*, which, like the parent noun *riot*, had been or was
about to be borrowed into English.

326. *Oriolus oriolus*. Anglo-Norman *orkoil* for the sake of the rhyme, but spelling
varies widely: *St John's E.17* (Acker 1993) offers *eywal*. English gloss *wodewale*
(see *OED* 'woodwall 1.; witwall 1.'). Adult humour again: 'cuckoo' suggests
cuckoldry both in Anglo-Norman and in English.

327. *Meles meles*. Anglo-Norman *tesschoun*; English gloss *brocke*.

328. Anglo-Norman *fen* (cf. later French *fiente*), which was to be borrowed into
English as *fen* (see *OED* 'fen n. 2' quotations 1340, 1387, 1460, 1513, 1535; *OED*
treats this as a use of an existing Old English word).

329. *Vulpes vulpes*. Anglo-Norman *gupil*; English gloss *fox*.

E maudist seit li mau putois,
Car, seit en vile ou en boys,
Ne fet fors mes k' il eit
812 Grace geleine a sun reheite.
E plus vaudreit un beleth
Pur fere ma graunge des raz neth
Ke totez les taupes de ci ki a Paris,
816 Ki funt taupaines en païs,
E meuz amase ensement,
Si jeo le huisse a talent,
Char de cerf ou de feoun
820 Ki chaunt de asne ou de poun.
E meuz aime kou de poun
Ki en l'escheker math de poun.
E de pooun la bele couwe
824 Doune delit a la veuwe.
Je vi ci desouz la dume
Un oisel plumé ci gist la plume,
Mes ki k'il seit ki l'ad plumé,
828 Meuz vodroie q'il ut nois bluché.

And a curse on the wicked polecat[330] because, in town or forest,
It never cares if only it has a fat hen for its pleasure;[331]
There's more worth in a weasel[332] to keep my barn free of rats[333]
Than all the moles[334] from here to Paris making their molehills in
    the earth;   816
Likewise better pile up, if I can call for what I want,
Meat of deer or fawn[335] than song of ass or peacock.[336]
But a lovely peacock's tail gives pleasure to the eye:
A lady prefers a peacock's tail to checkmate with a pawn.   824
Under a rosebush[337] I see a plucked bird: here's the feather,
But who plucked it? Better to have had a peeled[338] nut.

330. *Mustela putorius*. Anglo-Norman *putois*; English gloss *fulymard* (*OED* 'foumart').

331. English gloss *glading* (see *OED* 'gladding'). In the preceding phrase *grasse geleine*, English *fat hen*, 'fat' means 'fattened' (*OED* 'fat n. A. I. 1').

332. *Mustela nivalis*. Anglo-Norman *beleth* (modern French *belette*), one of the earliest recorded uses of this medieval euphemism ('pretty animal') for the earlier *mustela*. English gloss *wassele* (*OED* 'weasel').

333. *Rattus rattus*. Anglo-Norman *raz*, which is borrowed from a Germanic language; the same word *rat* was already known in English. Here, however, the English gloss is *ratonz* (see *OED* 'ratton'), which is borrowed from the alternative Anglo-Norman term *ratoun*.

334. *Talpa europaea*. English gloss *moldewarpes* (see *OED* 'mouldwarp'). In manuscript G the gloss is wrongly placed against *taupaine* 'molehill' rather than *taupe* 'mole' (Rothwell 2009, p. 37 note 8).

335. Anglo-Norman *feoun*, from which English *fawn* had already been borrowed.

336. *Pavo cristatus*. There is no need for a gloss, here or below: 'peacock' and 'pawn' were homonyms both in Anglo-Norman (*poun*) and in English (see *OED* 'pawn n.¹; pawn n.³').

337. Anglo-Norman *dume*. English gloss *brerebusk* (see *OED* 'brier, briar, brere n.¹ 5. briar-bush'. The only quotation (1562, Turner's *Herbal*) identifies this as the dog rose.

338. English gloss *polled, polt* (see *OED* 'palt v.¹; polt v.; pull v. I. 5. a').

Jeo vi ester un petit nein
Sur la river ke est dit Sein.
En sa main tent un heyn.
832   Pescher vout: ne pout pur ceyn.

Ore pur un charet descrivre le fraunceis

Pur un charret descrivere
Le fraunceis vous met en livere.
Dunc les reos vous di au primour,
836   Pus les wendeaus ki sunt entour.
Desouz les bendeaus, qe sunt de fer,
Sunt les jauntes attachez de fer.
En les jauntes entrent les rais,
840   E du solail issent les rais,
E de la mer veinent les raies,
E ver la feire vount les rais.
Mes les rais de charette
844   En les moyeaus ount lur recet.
Dit li moail de la reof
Tut dreit au mouwel de l'oef:
'Jeo su fort a fes porter'.
848   'E jeo', fest li autre, 'bon a manger'.
Mes en les moyeaus gist le essel
Ki par deuz heces se tient ouwel.
Les esseles unt lur juneres
852   Ki les eident cum bone freres.

I see a little dwarf standing beside the river Seine
With a hook[339] in his hand. He wants to fish, but he can't,
    because of the sleet.[340]   832

Now the French to describe a cart:

I shall put in your book the French to describe a cart:
I'll tell you the wheels first, then the tyres[341] around them;
Under the tyres, which are of iron, are the felloes, fixed with iron.
The spokes go into the felloes, beams shine from the sun,   840
Skates swim in the sea, burel is taken to the fair.[342]
But on a cart the spokes nest in the hub[343]
(The wheel-hub said to the egg-yolk:
'I'm strong enough to carry loads.' 'I'm good to eat,' the yolk
    replied).[344]   848
Now in the hubs lies the axle,[345] which is kept level by two pins;
The axles have their axle-clouts which help them like good
    brothers.

339. English gloss *angulhoc* (see *OED* 'angle n.^{1}; angle-hook').
340. The point of these lines is in the rhyme words, *nein* 'dwarf', *Sein* (but correctly *Seine*), *heyn* 'hook', *ceyn* (but correctly *ceim*) 'sleet'; also in the unrealized play on words (the dwarf might be fishing in the *Seine* with a *seine*; but no, he has a hook).
341. English gloss *bontes* (see *OED* 'bond n.^{1} I. 2. a' and compare 'band n.^{1} 4, 5; bend n.^{1} 2' and the heraldic term *bend*). The word *tire/tyre* was not yet in use. On the carting terminology see Sayers 2010e.
342. Homonyms in Anglo-Norman: *rai* 'spoke', *rai* 'ray, sunbeam', *raie* 'skate, ray', *rai* (elsewhere sometimes *drap de rai*) 'striped cloth'. The list is helped along by the fact that both spokes and rays radiate from a central hub. English glosses identify the fourth item as *bureus, birell clothes* (see *OED* 'burel 1'). This English word is borrowed from Anglo-Norman *burel* 'coarse striped cloth, often used for tables', which is the origin of *bureau* and is not independent of the heraldic term *barruly* (Anglo-Norman *borel*) 'striped'.
343. English gloss *nave, nathe* (see *OED* 'nathe; nave n.^{1}').
344. A play on words employing two meanings of Anglo-Norman *moyeau, moail, mouwel* 'wheel-hub, egg-yolk'.
345. English gloss *axetre* (see *OED* 'ax-tree').

Sur les esseiles gist le chartil,
E pur sauver le peril
Le chaltil est de becheus
856   Ferm liez a les esseus.
Entre le chartil e lé moyeaus
Sunt hurteuers trovez deus.
E chescune charet ki mene blez
860   Deit aver rideles au costez.
En les rideles vount roilouns
Par les trus, sanz nuls clavouns.
E si outre les moyeaus seent sauvers,
864   Dunc n'i faut sinoun eschelez.
Mes pur estre plus artillous,
Des esseaus plus vous dirroms.
Il ad essel e assel,
868   E li tierz ki ad a noun ascel.
Le chartil lyoms sur les esseaus;
En les moyeaus sunt les esseaus.
Mes les asceles avez vous
872   En ambesdeuz les bras a desouz.
En lymons veet li limoner
Ki adés porte le dosser,
E au ventre le ventrer,
876   E a la couwe le vauner.
Ventrer e ventrere i a,
Divers cum vous orrez ja.
Ventrere est proprement nomé
880   Une femme ke est demoeré
Pur eider en cas sa veisine
Quant ele girra en gysine;
Mes proprement dist hom ventrer
884   Qi au ventre porte li lymoner.

On the axle lies the cart-body, and to avoid accident
The cart-body is firmly fixed to the axles with straps.   856
Between the cart-body and the hub are found two hurters;[346]
And every cart that carries corn must have rails[347] at the sides;
Through the holes in the rails go rods,[348] without any nails.
Outside the hubs are clouts[349] which need no bells.   864
Now, to get more technical, we'll tell you more about the axles.
There's axles and hambarghs[350] and a third word, armpits;[351]
We rest the cart-body on the axles, the axles are in the hubs,
But you have armpits under both your arms.   872
The carthorse goes between the shafts.[352] It always wears a
        backstrap
And a belly-band[353] at its belly and a crupper[354] at its tail.
There's belly-band and midwife,[355] different, as you shall hear:
A midwife is the proper name for a woman who comes   880
To help her neighbour when it happens that she lies in
        childbirth,[356]
But people call belly-band what a carthorse wears around its belly.

346. Anglo-Norman *hurteuer*, from which English *hurter* (see *OED* 'hurter 2 1.')
     had already been borrowed; hence no gloss is needed.
347. English glosses *rathes, ronges* (see *OED* ' rathe n. 2; rung n.¹').
348. English gloss *staves* (see *OED* 'stave n.¹', where this sense is not specified).
349. English gloss *letheren clouts* (see *OED* 'wain-clout; clout n.¹ I. 2').
350. English gloss *hambrowes* (see *OED* 'hambargh; bargham; brecham'). Lines
     865–872 are not in manuscript T.
351. Three near-homonyms in Anglo-Norman: *essel* 'axle', *assel* or *escele* 'hambargh',
     ascel 'armpit'.
352. Anglo-Norman *limouner* 'carthorse', *lymons* 'shafts'; English gloss *thille hors*.
     See *OED* 'thill 1; thiller; thill-horse'.
353. English glosses *womberop, wam tow* (see *OED* 'womb n. 5. womb-rope;
     womb-tie, womb-tow').
354. Anglo-Norman *vauner*, an otherwise unknown word. English gloss *taylrop*
     (see *OED* 'tail-rope 1').
355. Cognates and near-homonyms in Anglo-Norman: *ventrer* 'belly-band',
     ventrere 'midwife', linked with *ventre* 'belly, womb'. Lines 877–884 are not
     in manuscript T.
356. English gloss *childing*.

Li traices ad la bracerole
Ki les lymons enbrace e cole.
Devant les braceroles sunt billez
888   Tailés de coteus ou de hachez.
Les couls dé chivaus portent esceles
E colers du quir en lur osseles.
En la charet est le somer,
892   La ou seet le charetter.
Si le charetter eit sa riorte
Dunt ces chivaus en curs resorte,
Dunc ad quanke li appent,
896   Kar ataunt suffist qeki l'entent.[7]
Mes pur estre plus sachaunt
Vous dirrai einz qe passe avant
Que en meyn tendra le charetter
900   E quei en mein avera le caruer.
Li charetter avera sa riorte,
Mes li carruer la aguilloun enporte,
E si li charetter estrile avera
904   Dunt ces chivaus counreera.
E li cotivers ne tine agaz
Ki ben ne frote de torcas
Einz qu'il seent enbeverez.
908   Mes au seir serrunt waez.

7.   For 893–896 T has: Ke teent en meyn la riorte *(a wippe)* Par unt le cheval a chemyn resorte.

The traces[357] have an eye[358] which embraces[359] and fixes the shafts;
In front of the eyes are pins whittled with a knife or a hatchet.[360]
Horses' necks wear hambarghs and leather collars on the hames.[361]   888
On the cart is the seat[362] where the carter sits,
And he uses his switch[363] to keep them on the right path.
But to be more informative I'll tell you what comes before,
What the carter will have in his hand and what the ploughman   896
    will have in his.
The carter will have his switch, but the ploughman takes his goad;
The carter will have a curry-comb[364] with which he'll curry[365] the
    horses,
And the farmer doesn't think it a joke[366] to rub the horses well   904
    with a wisp[367]
When they have been well watered. Then in the evening they will
    be waded:
There is a water-trough, so says the author, and he tells the truth,

357. Anglo-Norman *tres* (and in one manuscript *traices*), plural of *trait* 'draught'.
The Anglo-Norman plural is the source of the English singular word *trais*
(*OED* 'trace n.²') which is given here as a gloss.

358. English glosses *eyhe* (see *OED* 'eye n.¹ III. 21.' but no mention of this precise
sense), *hankes* (see *OED* 'hank n.').

359. English gloss *bicluppes* (see *OED* 'beclip v.¹').

360. Anglo-Norman *hachez*, which had evidently already been borrowed into
English (see *OED* 'hatchet n.'; the first citation there, 'before 1327', treats it
as a familiar word available for use in a metaphorical sense).

361. English gloss *homes* (see *OED* 'hame 2').

362. Anglo-Norman *somer*, which was borrowed into English in this and other
senses (see *OED* 'summer n.² 3. b.': *somer* is the spelling used in the 1523
citation).

363. English gloss +*haling wippe* (see note 151 above). This section is translated
from manuscript T, reducing the length by one couplet.

364. English gloss *horscome* (see *OED* 'horse-comb'). Lines 897–912 are not in
manuscript T.

365. Anglo-Norman *counreer*, which had already been borrowed into English (see
OED 'curry v.¹'); hence there is no gloss.

366. Anglo-Norman *gaz* (oblique case *gab*), which had already been borrowed into
English (see *OED* 'gab n.¹; gab v.¹'). English gloss *scorne*.

367. Anglo-Norman *torchas*. English gloss *wispe* (see *OED* 'wisp n.¹ 1. b').

Vayour i ad proprement,
Ceo dist li auctour ki ne ment,
Dunt les beofs e les chivaus sunt vaés,
912   E de tutes autres bestes sunt lavez.

Ore le fraunceis des propretez de carue

Puis ki deshore suffist du charret,
De la carue ore me entremet.
En la carue avez vous
916   Divers nouns e merveillous.
Primes le chef e le penoun,
Le manual e le tenoun.
Pardesouz est le oroilloun
920   E plus amount est l'escuchoun.
La soke ausi e le vomer
Avera carue de dever,
Mes war ki ne tuche
924   La zoke la zouche.

In which cattle and horses are waded and all other animals are
    washed.[368]

Now the French for the parts of a plough:

That's enough for the cart; I'll get to work on the plough.
On a plough you have many wonderful names:
First the share-beam[369] and the foot,[370] the handle and the
    crossbar,[371]
The plough-rest[372] underneath and the shield-board[373] above;
The plough must also have a coulter and a share,[374]
But be careful not to touch a tree-stump with the coulter.[375]

368. The distinction made here does not exist in English. 'Waded' in my translation
is almost an invented word, but not quite (see *OED* 'wade v. 6'). I use it to
translate the Anglo-Norman *waer, vaer* 'to wash (a horse)'. That word is
linked with *gué* 'ford', borrowed from Frankish **vad* but influenced by Latin
vadum. The English gloss in the manuscripts is *watred*, but this was a mistake,
a false friend: English *water* cannot mean 'wash', though it is cognate with
the Frankish and therefore with the Anglo-Norman.

369. Anglo-Norman *chef*, literally 'head'; English gloss *plou heved* (see *OED*
'plough-head'), which is probably not a loan-translation from Anglo-Norman,
since a comparable form *pflogis-houbit* exists in Old High German. On the
plough terminology see Sayers 2009f.

370. English gloss *foth* (see *OED* 'foot n. IV. 14; plough-foot' with variant forms
plowbat, plouhpote).

371. English gloss *stulte* (see *OED* 'stilt n.').

372. English gloss *ploureste* (see *OED* 'plough n.¹ 8. plough-rest, plough-ryst; reest
n.; wrest n.²').

373. Anglo-Norman *escuchoun*, literally 'shield'; English gloss *sheldebred* (see *OED*
'shield-board; shilboard'), perhaps influenced by the Anglo-Norman.

374. English gloss *shzar* (see *OED* 'share n.¹; ploughshare').

375. Wise advice suggested by near-homonymy: Anglo-Norman *zoke* 'coulter',
zouche 'stump'.

Enlonge la carue gist la haie,
Ki vent du boiz ou du haie.
La carue ad un maillet
928   E un moundilloun pur fere le neth.
Devaunt la claie sunt clavouns
Ou sunt atachez les tenouns.
Les boefs portent les jus
932   E pur Cristienes e pur Gius.
E par les arçzouns en jus fermés
Sunt les boefs cy forte artez
Ki les covent maugrer lour
936   Par le agoilloun eschuer errour.

Ore pur meisoun edifier

Si vous avez en penser
Mesoun ou chaumbre edefier,
Il covient au comencement
940   K'il eit bone fundament.
E puis leverez vous la mesere
Dunt femme est dit mesnere,

Along the plough lies the plough-beam [376] which comes from
    forest or hedge; [377]
The plough is equipped with a mallet [378] and a plough-staff [379] to
    clean it off;   928
In front of the beam are clevies [380] to fix the crossbars.
Oxen carry yokes for Christians and for Jews, [381]
And by the oxbows, fixed into a yoke, the oxen are so firmly
    restrained [382]
That in spite of themselves the goad guides them.   936

Now for building a house:

If you have in mind to build a house or room
You must start by laying a foundation,
And then you raise the house-wall (whence a woman is called
    housewife): [383]

---

376. English gloss *plougbem* (see *OED* 'beam n.' I. 5.; plough-beam').
377. Not really from a hedge: homonyms in Anglo-Norman, *haie* (modern French *age, haie*) 'plough-beam', *haie* 'hedge'.
378. Anglo-Norman *maillet*, diminutive of *maille*. English gloss *plou betel* (see *OED* 'plough n.' 8. plough-beetle'), a term afterwards replaced by *plough-mell*, in which the second element is borrowed from Anglo-Norman *maille*.
379. English glosses *kirstaf* and *ploustare*; see *OED* 'plough-staff'.
380. See *OED* 'clevis'.
381. Near-homonyms in Anglo-Norman: *jus* (singular *jug*) 'yokes'; *Guis* (singular *Guif*) 'Jews'.
382. English gloss *streingned* (see *OED* 'strain v.' I. 1., 4.').
383. The purpose of this unexpected aside is to introduce a three-way homonymy, *mesere* 'house wall', *mesuere* 'housewife', *messere* 'hayward'. Walter is etymologically wrong in that the Anglo-Norman words for 'house wall' and 'housewife' are not cognates. The first derives from Latin *maceria* 'wall', the second is in the word family of *mansio* and *mansura*. On the house-building terminology, see Sayers 2010c.

    The text is not (I think) trying to say that a woman is in charge of the house as opposed to the courtyard. In context that would not be true: she was in charge of both the *maison* and the *basse-cour*.

Car ceste est mur q'enclost la curte,
944 E mesere ou coumble aourt.
Mes il i ad messer e mesere.
Entendez en diverse manere!
Ly messere ad li chaumpe en cure,
948 Mes mesere fet mesoun sure.
Sur la mesere en travers outre
Amount le celer mettez le poutre.
Au pieler desouz le poutre
952 De chevestre liez le poutre.
E en vostre soler desuz le poutre
Trestuz les seillouns mettez outre.
E desuz les seillouns la plauncié,
956 De bordes ou de plastre pavié.
Sur la mesere les traes mettez.
De deuz cheverouns un couple facez
Ki ferme estera sur la mesere
960 Par kivil e par terere.
Dunc n'i faut si coumble noun.
Ou tut amount la meisun
Covient enlunge aver grenchour,
964 Dunc le cumble ert mult plus sur.
Pur ceo fetes le cumble apert,
E qu'il seit trop bien couvert.
Mes pur plus avaunt parler,
968 Vous ne devez ublier
K'il encovent aver grenchouns
E clous ficchez en vos mesouns.
E trenchons a la meisoun ausi.
972 Car pur aprise le vous die,

A yard-wall encloses a courtyard but it's a house-wall[384] on which
    the roof rests.   944
But there's hayward and wall: listen to their differences!
The hayward looks after fields but a wall keeps the house safe.
In the wall, crosswise, above the cellar fix the beam;[385]
(To a pillar under the beam tie the filly by its halter;)[386]   952
For your flooring above the beam lay all the joists,
And on the joists the floor, paved with boards[387] or plaster.
On the wall put the rafters:[388] two rafters make a couple[389]
And are fixed firm on the wall by nail and auger.   960
All that's needed is a roof. But on the very top of the house
There must be a roof-beam,[390] lengthwise, and thus the roof will
    be much more secure:
So open up the roof to close it down better!
To continue, you mustn't forget   968
That your houses should have laths[391] and fixed nails;
There must be splints[392] in the house too. I mention this for
    information

384. The distinction made here does not exist in modern English: Anglo-Norman
mur 'courtyard wall', *mesere* 'house wall, esp. end-wall'. For the latter the
English glosses are *helewoth* and *wowe* (see *OED* 'helewou; wough n.¹').

385. English glosses *wivertre* (see *OED* 'wiver¹') and *giste-tre* (see *OED* 'joist n.¹;
joist-tree').

386. Homonyms in Anglo-Norman: *poutre* 'main beam', *poutre* 'filly'.

387. Anglo-Norman *borde*, borrowed from Frankish, needed no translation as it
was paralleled by English *board*. I am grateful to William Sayers' notes for
help with these lines.

388. Anglo-Norman *cheveron*, which was to be borrowed into English, but usually
had the sense of the V shape made by a couple of rafters.

389. Anglo-Norman *couple*, borrowed into English in this sense (see *OED* 'couple
n. II. 8.') and in others.

390. Anglo-Norman *genchour*; English gloss +*pantre*. Lines 963–980 are not in
manuscript T.

391. Anglo-Norman *grenchouns*, in origin a spelling variant of *genchour* above.

392. Anglo-Norman *trenchons*; English glosses *splentes*, *splentres*, +*lynthes*. Exactly
what these are is not clear. In *Femina trenchoms a pareie* is glossed +*stantyz to
walle*.

Mes chescun home ne seet pas
K'il eit difference en ceo cas,
Car trenchons funt a mesoun eese,
976 E trenchesouns a plusur despleise,
E a chivaus nomeement.
Trenchesouns apel hom proprement.
Uncore fest plus a saver
980 Endreit de meisoun edifier.
De dreit dever i covent estre
Li aumeire e la fenestre.
Aumeire e aumaire i a.
984 A l'aumere fume istra,
Car en fraunceis est aumere nomé
Ki ci est 'lover' appelee.
Mes ceo est proprement aumaire
988 Ou l'em mette viaunde e viaire.
A l'entré del hus est la lyme,
E outre la teste est la sullime.
Decoste sunt gymeaus deus
992 Ou sunt ficchez les aneaus.
En un gymel sunt les gouns
Si deuz verteveles eoms
Ore fetes cliké en serrure.
996 Si ert la meisun plus sure.

Because not everyone knows the difference between these two:
Splints ease the house, but gripes[393] give trouble to many,   976
And the term is properly used of horses in particular.
There's still more to know about building a house:
There properly needs to be a louver[394] and a window.
There's louver and cupboard:[395] smoke comes out of the louver,   984
Because the French *aumeire* is what is called 'louver' over here,
While an *aumaire* is properly where you put meat and
        provisions.[396]
At the doorway is the threshold[397] and overhead is the lintel;[398]
At the sides are two doorposts[399] to which rings are fixed.   992
In one doorpost are the hinge-hooks,[400] with two hingles in
        them.[401]
So drop the latch into the staple, and the house will be safe.

393. Apparent cognates in Anglo-Norman: *trenchons* 'splints', *trenchesouns* 'gripes'.
    For the latter the English gloss is *gnawinges* (*OED* 'gnawing vbl.n.').
394. English glosses *smoke-hole*, *lover*, the latter included by Walter in the text a
    few lines below (see *OED* 'louvre 1'). In its oldest English use *louver* meant
    'smoke-hole', a structure which, as eventually elaborated, took the name
    chimney. Both *louver* and *chimney* are 14th-century loanwords from French
    or Anglo-Norman; the native compound *smoke-hole* is also first recorded in
    the 14th century.
395. Anglo-Norman *aumeire*, *aumaire*, spelling variants of the same word. In the
    sense 'pantry' it was soon to be borrowed into English (see *OED* 'ambry').
    Lines 983–988 are not in manuscript T.
396. Anglo-Norman *viaire*; English glosses *drynke* (a mistake), *lyflode* (see *OED*
    'livelihood 1 2.').
397. English gloss *therswalde*, close to the old English forms of the word.
398. In Anglo-Norman the two are cognate, *lyme* 'threshold', *sullyme* 'lintel'.
    English glosses *hoverdorne*, *overslay* (see *OED* 'overdorne; durn; overslay').
399. Anglo-Norman *gemel*, soon to be borrowed into English in the sense 'hinge'
    (see *OED* 'gemel 5.'), but here the gloss is correctly *dorstode* (see *OED* 'door-
    stead').
400. English gloss *hoke*.
401. Rings that fit over the hinge-hooks, forming a hinge. Anglo-Norman *vertevele*.
    English glosses *hengles*, *bondes of hokes*, *twisten* (see *OED* 'hingle; band n.¹ 3.;
    twist n.¹ I. 1.'). I am grateful to William Sayers for letting me see his unpub-
    lished translation of the house-building passage.

Ore pur attirere le fu

Fetez ore prest apparailler,
Ki nous puissoms tost manger.
Une valet de vous quatre
1000   Va toust munder cele astre.
Portez les cendres au fimer.
Les asteles fetes anlumer
Par un tysoun de fu enpris
1004   Ki de la quisine serra pris.
Les asteles mettez en travers
Les chenés furchez de fers.
Si des osceles du chival
1008   Facez asteles, vos frés mal.
Mettez au fu astele du cheine,
Coupé de aune ou de freyne,
E va dunc quere la fue,
1012   Quir enclowé de fust de feu.
Mes pur la verdour des asteles
Jeo ne vei issir estenceles.
Va quere breses en un teske.
1016   Attirez le feu, si vient l'eveske.
Ore agardez, beau duce frere,
Ne averez tost belechere.
Gardez vos dras des flammecches;
1020   Mettez en breses peires e pesces.

Now to make up the fire:

> Now make things ready so that we can eat soon.
> One of you four boys will sweep out the hearth. 1000
> Take the ashes to the dungheap;[402] light the kindling[403]
> With a burning brand fetched from the kitchen.
> Place the kindling across the andirons[404] (forged in iron).
> You can make your kindling from hambarghs but it's a bad idea.[405] 1008
> Put oak kindling in the fire or cut it from alder or ash.[406]
> Go and find the bellows, leather enclosed in beech-wood.
> If you spare the wind of the bellows you'll be taken for a fool.[407]
> But because of the greenness[408] of the kindling I don't see any
>   sparks coming:
> Go and get embers in a shard and build up the fire: the bishop's
>   coming.[409] 1016
> Now take care, dear brother, or you will soon lose your
>   cheerfulness:
> Keep your clothes away from the flames:[410] put pears and peaches
>   in the embers.

402. English gloss *mochul* (see *OED* 'muck-hill').

403. Anglo-Norman *asteles*. English gloss *szhides* (see *OED* 'shide n.'), usually meaning 'splinters of timber'. The sense wanted here is more general; following Kennedy's suggestion, I use 'kindling'.

404. Anglo-Norman *chenés* (literally 'little dogs'), source of the much later English loan-translation *fire-dog*. The English gloss here is *aundhirnes*, a word which had already been borrowed from Anglo-Norman (see *AND* 'aundire, aundirne'; *OED* 'andiron').

405. You would only do it for the sake of a play on words: *astele* 'chip', *escele* or *oscele* 'hambargh, horse-collar'.

406. Why these three species? Oak, Anglo-Norman *chene*, is perhaps suggested by the preceding *chenés* 'firedogs'; ash, Anglo-Norman *frene*, rhymes with it.

407. Near-homonyms in Anglo-Norman: *feu* 'beech', *fue* 'bellows', *fu* 'fire', *fust* 'wood', *fou* 'fool'. The English gloss for the last is *fool*, already familiar as a loanword from Anglo-Norman. This couplet is added from manuscript T.

408. English gloss *grenhed* (see *OED* 'greenhead 1').

409. For the sake of the rhyme: Anglo-Norman *teske* 'shard', *veske* 'bishop'.

410. English gloss *huysseles* (see *OED* 'isel, izle').

Ore pur attirer bel la mesoun

Moundés la mesoun, si la jungez.
Asseez la table, si la coverez.
Les bous de la table e les cures
1024 Coverez de nape devaunt seignurs.
Au meins ki ceo point seit estable,
De blaunche nape coverez la table.
E la secunde ausi coverez
1028 De blaunche nape, si vous l'eez.
E si la nape seit trop sale,
N'est mie avenaunt en sale,
Kar blaunche nape mult usé
1032 Vaut plus ke novele enboulré.
Lavés les hanapes, mundez les queles,
Coupés des cysours dé ungles les eles.
Va t'en, quistroun, ou toun havez
1036 Estrere le hagis del postnez.
E mettez vostre veille rouche
Desuz vos pos, noun pas la louche.
Priez Jonet ki ta coyfe i leuche
1040 De un lucchere suiz la louche,
E mettez la teille a l'ydol de lith
Prés de la rose qe ja enflestrith.
Mes a la vile rouche redirroms,
1044 Ou plus aprendre i pouns.
La rouche server deit des ees,
Dount nous veom voler les dees,
E un par sei singulerement
1048 *An hony bee* est proprement,
E proprement un dé des ees
En engleis est *a suarme of bees.*

Now to tidy up the house:

> Clean the house and spread with rushes; set up the table and
>   cover it.
> Cover the ends and sides of the table before lords; 1024
> At least let this be agreed, cover the table with a white tablecloth.
> Cover the second,[411] too, with a white tablecloth if you have one.
> If the tablecloth is too dirty it isn't suitable for the hall;
> A white tablecloth, much worn, is better than a new but dirty[412]
>   one. 1032
> Wash the cups, clean the bowls, cut the agnails[413] from your nails
>   with scissors;
> Off you go, scullion! With your flesh-hook take the haggis[414] out
>   of the pot.
> You can put your old beehive under your feet, but not the ladle,
> And ask Janet to slick[415] your hair with the slickstone[416] on the
>   sideboard. 1040
> And put a cloth over the bedside figurine[417] beside the rose that's
>   already faded;[418]
> But let's talk again about the old hive: there we can learn more.
> The hive must be for bees; we want the swarms to fly into it,
> Because one on its own is properly *an hony bee*, 1048
> While *un dees de ees* is in English *a suarme of bees*,

411. Anglo-Norman *la secunde* 'the second table'. In early 19th-century English
   this was the servants' table (see *OED* 'second a. and n.² A. 7. second table').
   Lines 1025–1028 are not in manuscript T.
412. English gloss *biselet* (see *OED* 'besoiled').
413. Anglo-Norman *eles* (literally 'wings'). English glosses *wottewale, angenayle*
   (see *OED* 'wartwale; agnail').
414. Anglo-Norman *hagis*, thought to be a loanword from English.
415. English gloss *szhike* (see *OED* 'slick v.; sleek v.').
416. English glosses *szhikinston, slykston* (see *OED* 'slickstone; sleekstone'). Near-
   homonyms in Anglo-Norman: *louche* 'ladle', *leuche* 'slick' and its cognate
   lucchere 'slickstone', *rouche* 'beehive', *huche* 'sideboard'.
417. I can't explain this. Nor can the writer of the English gloss in manuscript T,
   who writes *the cloth ate beddes heved* '[put] the sheet over the bedhead'.
418. English gloss *welwit* (see *OED* 'wallow v. 2').

E c'est une brecche de mel nomé
1052   Ki en la rouche funt les ees de gré.

Ore pur diverse paroles

Requillez genz bel a manger.
Si poez meimes alloser.
Taillez ceo pain que est paré.
1056   Les bisseaus seient pur Deu doné.
Du cotel trenchoms les bisseaus.
Du quiller mangoms mieaus.
Frussés ceo pain qi vent de fourn.
1060   Debrusés cel os de venour.
Rumpés la cord qe fet nusaunce.
Enfreinés covenaunt de deceivaunce.
Partiez, valet, en vos escous
1064   Le haranc sor de frahel rous,
Kar par devaunt sunt vos escous
E d'encoste sunt vos gerouns.
E donez tost a celui pelryn
1068   Ke porte un chape de hermin.
Cy vint un garzoun esclavoté.
La pruve vous ert ja mustré,
Kar trop avera des esclavos
1072   Ki du chivaul suwe les esclos.

And a honeycomb[419] is the name for what bees like to make in
  their hive.[420]

Now various words:

Get people together for a meal; you can even do them honour in
  this way.
Slice this loaf that has been pared;[421] the crusts[422] should be given
  for alms.[423]   1056
Let's chop the crusts with a knife; let's eat the crumbs with a
  spoon.
Break this loaf that's come from the oven; break this bone from
  the huntsman;
Break the cord that's in our way; break[424] the agreement
  deceitfully.
Share out from your lap, boy, the red pickled herring in the basket 1064
(It's your skirt in front, your gores[425] at your side)
And give some quickly to this pilgrim who's wearing an ermine
  cap.
Here comes a mud-spattered boy:[426] as you'll soon see
He has lots of splashes from following the horse's hooves.[427]   1072

---

419. English gloss *honny come* (see *OED* 'comb n.¹ 8.; honeycomb'). On the bee-
  keeping terms see Sayers 2009c. Lines 1043–1052 are not in manuscript T.
420. A series of jingling phrases in Anglo-Norman and English, *un dé de ees, a
  suarme of bees, funt les ees de gré* 'bees like to do', *server deit des ees* 'must be
  for bees'.
421. Anglo-Norman *parer* 'prepare', and here specifically 'pare, trim', already
  borrowed into English in this sense (see *OED* 'pare v.¹ II. 3.').
422. English gloss *paringes* (see *OED* 'paring', based on the verb *pare*: see previous
  note).
423. 'For God', according to manuscript G.
424. *Fruisser, debriser, rumper, enfreindre*: four Anglo-Norman verbs that can be
  translated 'break' in English.
425. Anglo-Norman *escous, escurs* 'lap, skirt' and *geroun* 'gore'. Lines 1065–1066
  are not in manuscript T.
426. English glosses +*bispirnit, be[s]quirt* (see *OED* 'bespurt, besquirt').
427. English gloss *steppes* (apparently imprecise, but cf. *OED* 'step n.¹ I. 11').

[137]

Fens estreit de puaunt souz
Fest sale nape e grace chouz.
E herbe qe crest al huis del estable
1076   Fet blaunche nape e megre table.
Deus garzouns chacent grant preie;
A chescun mot l'un baubeye
E li autre ne peut parler
1080   Une parole sanz nascier.
Mes ne me chaut s'il nascie,
Kar il ne vaut pas un aillie.
E ki meins vaut, il baave tut dis.
1084   Si crere vousist moun avis,
Il enpriereit sa mere
Ki ele le feise un baavvere.
Mes veez, si vient Mestre Huge,
1088   Ki ren ne parle si il ne buge.
Mes de femmes ai dedeing grant
Ki par orgoille se aforcent tant
En parler bleser tut dis
1092   Pur meuz pleiser a lur amis.
Ausi ad il tusser e escouper,
Ruper, vomer e esternuer.

Dung taken from a stinking midden [428] makes dirty [429] tablecloth
    and fat cabbages;
Grass growing at the stable door makes white tablecloth and lean
    table.
Two boys are chasing a big prey; at each word one stammers [430]
And the other can't say a word without sniffing, [431]   1080
But I don't care if he sniffs because he isn't worth a clove of
    garlic [432]
And what's worse, he slobbers [433] all the time. If he took my advice
He'd ask his mother to make him a bib.
Look: here comes master Hugh, who never says anything without
    stuttering! [434]
I have great disdain for women who through pride take care   1088
When speaking to lisp [435] all the time to please their lovers.
Also there's cough and spit, belch, spew and sneeze.

428. English glosses *muk hul* ('muckhill', see note 402 above), *pludde* (see *OED*
    'plud; puddle').
429. English gloss *soly* (see *OED* 'soily a.1 3').
430. English gloss *wlaf* (see *OED* 'wlaffe').
431. Anglo-Norman *nascier*. English gloss *snyvele* (see *OED* 'snivel v. 1').
432. In manuscript T he isn't worth *un escarie*, an unknown word, possibly meant
    for *un escarbot*, because the English gloss *starebodde* is the same word in
    origin, meaning a dung-beetle (see *OED* 'scarbot').

        In manuscript G the Anglo-Norman is *ne vaut pas un aillie* 'isn't worth
    anything'; but literally *un aillie* means either 'a clove of garlic' or 'a service-
    berry' (see also notes 272–273). The English gloss is *a pile of garlec*. This precise
    sense of *pile* is not otherwise recorded. Comparison of the *OED* entries 'pile
    n.1 2. a., c.; pill n.1 a. (citation 1388); pill v.1 II. 5 (citation 1440); pilled 1.
    (citation *c.* 1420); garlic n. (citation 1522)' suggests that the meaning intended
    in English is 'skin of a garlic clove'.
433. English gloss *slavereth* (see *OED* 'slabber v.; slaver v.; slobber v.').
434. English gloss *stotteth* (see *OED* 'stut v.1').
435. English gloss *wlispen* (see *OED* 'lisp v.; wlisp a.'). Lines 1095–1104 are not in
    manuscript T.

Home dist qu'il tousse de dreit
1096   Ki mout de ruge serveise beit;
E cil qui trop laumbei au quer
Sovent li esteut escouper.
E cil qe mouche masche ou gouste
1100   Un grant gate li mettez jouste,
Car ruper li esteut tresben
Ou il vomera maugré soen.
Mes esternnuer sovent
1104   Saunté est e aleggement.

A man who's drunk a lot of red beer [436] may just cough   1096
And when a man is sick [437] to his heart he'll often only spit,
But a man who chews or swallows a fly throws up a bowlful;
Belching would do very well but he spews in spite of himself.
Yet sneezing is often healthy and cheering.   1104

436. English gloss *cer*, apparently an abbreviated form of *servoise*. The Anglo-Norman *serveise* was to be borrowed into English, but was rarely used (see *OED* 'servoice'; Rothwell 2009, p. 50 note 9).
437. English gloss *wamblez* (see *OED* 'wamble v.').

The High Feast (MS T)

812   Un vallet de la novelerie
       Vynt her de une mangerie
       E de la feste nous ad countee
       Coment lour service fut araee.
816   Saunz payn e vin hou cerveyse
       Ne serreit nul a feste a heyse.
       Mes tous tres y out ellyz
       Il nous aveyent diz.
820   Au primour fut aporté
       La teste du sengler enarmé,

The High Feast (Trinity College, Cambridge, MS O.2.21)

A young man of fashion came here from a dinner   812
And told us about the feast, how the service was arranged.[438]
Without bread and wine or beer[439] no feast will be comfortable;
But they had all three, they told us.
At the beginning was served boar's head well armed[440]   820

438. As explained in the introduction (p. 29) the High Feast has been translated from manuscripts T and G separately. This section has been discussed in detail by Constance Hieatt (1982) and an edition and translation appears in Hieatt and Butler 1985, pp. 2–4.

439. This rule is more economical than the equivalent in manuscript G ('without bread, wine and beer').

440. Anglo-Norman *la teste du sengler enarmée*; English gloss *bores heved*, and in another manuscript *the heved of þe boor yarmed*. It is presented still armed with its tusks. The same participle, Anglo-Norman *enarmé* and English *armed*, is elsewhere used in the sense 'larded [with bacon]': *Feast Menus Swanne henarmez ... Pecok enarmez* (in Jefferson 1998); *Ancient Cookery Craunes and Herns shall be armed with larde* (*Household Ordinances* 1790, as cited in *OED*). I find that unlikely here: would one lard a boar's head? Tobler and Lommatzsch's translation 'in plenty' (cited by Rothwell 2009, p. 93 note 3) also does not fit: you don't have plenty of boar's head: either you have one or you haven't.

E au groyn le coler enbaneree.
E pus veneysoun ho la formentee.
824 Assez parmy la mesoun
De grece e de enfermeysoun.
E pus aveyent diversetés en rost,
Sys checun, autre de cost
828 Gruhes e pouns e cynes,
Houhes rosers, purceus e gelynes.

The snout [441] with the neck [442] garlanded, [443] then venison [444] with
    frumenty. [445]
About the house there was plenty of grice [446] and fermison. [447]
Then there were various meats roasted, six dishes each and more
    on the side,
Cranes, peacocks and swans, marsh-geese, [448] sucking-pigs [449] and   828
    hens;

441. Anglo-Norman *groin*, probably already borrowed into English in this sense
    (see *OED* 'groin n.¹ 2.').

442. Anglo-Norman *coler*, a word already known in English but apparently not in
    this sense, which is first noted in 1610 (see *OED* 'collar n. 19. a'). However,
    there is no English gloss.

443. Anglo-Norman *enbaneree*. English gloss *with baneres of floures* (see *OED*
    'banner n.¹', but this sense is not given).

444. Anglo-Norman *venesoun* 'meat of four-legged game', already borrowed into
    English in the same sense (see *OED* 'venison n. 1. a.'), and already (pace
    OED) beginning to focus on deer – as seems to be the case here, since boar
    and rabbit are named separately.

445. Anglo-Norman *formenté*, soon to be borrowed into English (if it was not
    already) in the form *furmenty* (see *OED* 'frumenty, furmety 1. β.'). The first
    citation in *OED* is to the recipe in the *Forme of Cury* (see now Hieatt and
    Butler 1985, p. 98); there is another contemporary recipe in *Diversa Servicia*
    (Hieatt and Butler 1985, p. 62). Frumenty was a typical accompaniment to
    venison. So *c.* 1460, in John Russell's *Boke of Nurture*, *Fatt venesoun with
    frumenty* (line 383: Furnivall 1868).
        Rothwell (2009, p. 93 note 8) suggests French *fromentel*, which Godefroy
    glosses '*vin fromentel, vin fait avec du fromenteau*' – wheat beer, in other
    words. That suggestion is unnecessary in view of the citations already given
    showing that venison was served with frumenty.

446. Young game such as kids and piglets taken out of season. Anglo-Norman *gres*,
    a borrowing from Old English (see *OED* 'grice 1').

447. Venison taken in the close season. Anglo-Norman *enfermisoun, fermeyson*,
    borrowed into English about this date (see *OED* 'fermison'), though the
    English gloss in manuscript T explains more simply: *take out of time*. Compare
    the alliterative *Morte Arthure*: *Flesch fluriste of furmysone with frumentee noble*
    (line 180: Brock 1871).

448. See note 318.

449. Anglo-Norman *purceau*; English gloss *porceau* (not in *OED*, but cf. 'porket,
    porkin, porkling, porkrel').

Au ters aveyent conys en gravé
E viande de Cypre enfoundree
832 De maces e kubibes e clous doree,
Vin blaunke e vermayl a grant plentee,

As third course [450] they had rabbits [451] in gravy [452] and *Viaunde de Cypre* [453] steeped, [454]

Mace, cubebs and gilded cloves, [455] white and red wine in plenty;   832

450. Anglo-Norman *au ters.*

451. Anglo-Norman *conin,* already borrowed into English as *coning* (see *OED* 'cony, coney').

452. Anglo-Norman *gravé.* The word was soon to be borrowed into English (if it was not already) in the form *gravey* (see *OED* 'gravy 1.' and Spitzer 1944). See the recipe *La manere coment l'en deit fere gravee,* which suggests *conyns* 'rabbits' as a possible main ingredient for the dish, in the Anglo-Norman recipe collection *Coment l'en deit fere viande e claree* (Hieatt and Jones 1986, pp. 866, 877). There is a recipe specifically for *Conynggez in grave* in *Ordinance of Pottage* no. 32: *Perboile connynggez in gode brothe; take them up. Smyte them in pexis; make hem clene. Do hem in a pott with hole clowis, macis, & onions, ycutt sommdel grete, & pouuder. Blaunche almondys; grynde hem & drawe up withe the same brothe a thike mylke, & do togedyr, & suger. Boyle hit. Loke hit be salt; messe hit forthe. Cast theron a dragge of clowys, macys, and mynsyd gynger and blaunch poudyr* (Hieatt 1988, p. 46). See also note 465.

453. There is a recipe in *BL Royal 12.C.xii: Viaunde de Cypre. Let d'alemaunz, flur de rys, poudre de gyngyvre si qu'il fleyre bien de le gyngyvre; e qu'il soit plaunté de gyngebras ou festicade; colour, jaune* 'Food of Cyprus. Almond milk, rice flour, ground ginger to give a good aroma of ginger; it should be decorated with "gingerbread" and ground pistachio nuts; the color, yellow' (text and translation in Hieatt and Jones 1986). For the same recipe in Middle English in *Diversa Cibaria* see Hieatt and Butler 1985, p. 48. Further citations in the same volume and in *MED* s.v. 'viaund(e)'.

454. Anglo-Norman *enfoundree,* coated or steeped in honey or sugar syrup. When the word is re-used in the revised Feast (below), sugar is specified.

455. These were extremely expensive spices, all three of them imported over a great distance from far beyond the direct geographical knowledge of medieval Europe; cubebs from Java, mace and cloves from the Moluccas (Dalby 2000, pp. 53–55). The cloves are made still more costly and luxurious by gilding.

E pus aveyent fesaunz e ascyez e perdriz,
Grives e alouhes e plovers ben rostiz,

Pheasants, woodcocks, partridges, fieldfares, larks, plovers [456] well roasted,

456. *Charadrius pluvialis*. Anglo-Norman *plover*, already borrowed into English (see *OED* 'plover'). Fifteenth-century instructions for *Fesaunt rost* and *Plouer rost* are found in Bodleian Douce 55. *Fesaunt rost: Lete a fesaunt blode in the mouth, and lete hym blede to deth; & pulle hym, and draw hym, & kutt a-wey the necke by the body, & the legges by the kne, & perbuille hym, & larde hym, and putt the knese in the vent: and rost hym, & reise hym vpp, hys legges & hys wynges, as off an henne; & no sauce butt salt ... Plouer rost: Breke the skulle of a plouere, & pull hym drye, and draw hym as a chike, and cutte the legges and the wynges by the body, and the heued and necke allso, & roste hym, and reyse the legges and wynges as an henne: and no sauce butt salt* (Austin 1888, pp. 116–117).

836 E braun e crespes e friture
Ho zukre roset poudré la temprure.

Brawn,[457] crisps [458] and fritters [459] with powdered rose-sugar [460] as corrective;[461]

457. English *braon* has already appeared above with the meaning 'calf of the leg', and Anglo-Norman *braon* with the meaning 'muscle'. To judge by the immediate context the meaning here is not simply 'flesh meat' (Hieatt and Butler 1985, p. 173), nor yet 'skin, crackling' (as in *OED* 'brawn n. 3. [citation 1570]') but offcuts from the roast – meat or skin – as a delicacy. In one of the menus edited in Hieatt and Butler 1985 (p. 39) *brokon brawne* occurs with *fretowrys* (see note 459) at a similar point in the meal.

458. Anglo-Norman *crespes*, soon to be borrowed into English, if it was not already. See *OED* 'crisp n. 3.': 'a crisp kind of pastry made by dropping batter into boiling fat.' The English word occurs in *Diversa Servicia* and in the *Forme of Cury* (Hieatt and Butler 1985, pp. 67, 136); it is the same in origin as modern French *crêpes*, which are indeed, from the viewpoint of a scriptorium in Oxford, 'a crisp kind of pastry made by dropping batter into boiling fat' – but not too much of it.

459. Anglo-Norman *fruture*, unexpectedly singular to rhyme with *temprure*. The word was soon to be borrowed into English if it was not already (see *OED* 'fritter n.¹ 1.'). *Fretowrys* occur at a similar point in the meal in two of the menus edited in Hieatt and Butler 1985 (pp. 39, 41), in one case alongside *brokon brawne* (see note 457). John Russell's *Boke of Nurture* (Furnivall 1868) lists three types: *frutur viant, frutur sawge* and *frutur powche*.

460. Anglo-Norman *zukre roset*. The first word, 'sugar', was already borrowed into English as *zuker, sucar* etc. The second was soon to be borrowed into English if it was not already (see *OED* 'roset a. 1. a. sugar roset'; the first citation in *OED* is from 1398 in Trevisa's translation of *Bartholomaeus Anglicus de proprietatibus rerum*, which describes *succura rosacia, suger rosette that hath vertu to comforte and to binde*. Earlier than this, *sugre roset* is called for in a recipe for *Browet de Almayne* in *Utilis coquinario* (Hieatt and Butler 1985, p. 87).

461. Anglo-Norman *temprure*, soon to be borrowed into English if it was not already (see *OED* 'temperure 1.'; the first citation is from Wyclif's Bible translation, *Ezekiel* 13.14). The meaning is that rose-sugar acts as a spice, correcting the dietary qualities (and, incidentally, the flavours) of food.

Aprés manger aveyent a graunt plentee
Blaunche poudre ho la grose dragee.

The High Feast (MS G)

Ore le fraunceis pur un feste araer

Un vallet de la noveilerie
Ki vint her de un mangerie,
E de la feste nous ad cunté
1108   Cum lur servise fust araé.
Saunt pain, vin e cerveise
Ne serreint nuls a feste a ese.
Mes tut treis mout en liz
1112   Il en hurent, nos ad diz.
Mes de autre feste a parlé
Des cours k'il urent au manger.
Primes la teste de sengler ben armé
1116   E le groin plein banneré.
Puis venesoun ové la formenté
Puis meinte autre diverseté.
Grues, poeuns e cynes,
1120   Chevereaus, purceaus e gelines,
Puis averent conins en gravé,
Trestut de zugre enfundré,

And when the table was removed, blanch powder[462] as whole
    sweetmeats.

The High Feast (University Library, Cambridge, MS Gg.1.1)

Now the French for arranging a feast:

A young man of fashion came here from a dinner
And told us about the feast, how the service was arranged.   1108
Without bread, wine and beer[463] no feast will be comfortable,
But they had as much as they wanted of all three, the boy told us.
He talked about another feast and the courses[464] they had to eat.
First the boar's head well armed and the snout fully garlanded,   1116
Then venison with frumenty and many other varied things :
Cranes, peacocks and swans, kids, sucking-pigs and hens ;
Then they had rabbits in gravy, all coated in sugar,[465]

462. Anglo-Norman *blaunche poudre*, soon to be borrowed into English if it was
not already. See the recipe *To make blawnce pouder* in *Goud Kokery* (Hieatt
and Butler 1985, p. 153): it calls for *a half lb. suger and ii unc gynger* root,
pounded and ground together so fine that the mixture does not crunch
between the teeth. For later evidence see *OED* 'blanch a. 1'. The first citation
for 'blanch powder' there is *c.* 1460 in John Russell's *Boke of Nurture* : *aftur
sopper, rosted apples, peres, blanch powder, your stomak for to ese* (line 122:
Furnivall 1868). The blanch powder might be sprinkled on the apples, as in
Cogan's *Haven of Health* (1636 edition): *A very good blanch powder, to strow
upon rosted apples.*

463. See note 439.

464. Anglo-Norman *cours*, already borrowed into English in this sense in the form
cours (see *OED* 'course n. V. 26.'). The word is not used in the Trinity version
of the Feast, though several courses are specified: see note 450.

465. On the rabbits in gravy see note 452. In the Trinity Feast the sugar appeared
in a different context. However, the first citation for 'gravy' in *OED*, in the
Forme of Cury, is a recipe for exactly what Walter specifies here, *Connynges in
gravey* [with sugar]: *Take connynges: smite hem to pecys; perboile hem and drawe
hem with a gode broth, with almaundes, blaunched and brayed. Do therinne
sugur, and powdour gynger, and boyle it and the flesshe therwith; flour it with
sugur and with powdour gynger and serve forth* (Hieatt and Butler 1985, p. 104).
A similar recipe appears in *Diversa servicia* (ib., p. 63).

Maces, quibibes e clous gilofrez,
1124 E autre espicerie ascez,
Viaunde de Cypre e maumerie,
Vin vermaile e blaunc a plenté,
Puis i out autre foysen de roste,
1128 Checun de eus autre encouste -
Feyzauns, asciez e perdriz,
Grives, alawes e plovers rostiz,
Braoun, crispes e fruture
1132 Ové zucre roset la temprure.
E quant la table fust ousté,
Blaunche poudre en grose dragé,
E de autre noblei au foisoun.
1136 Einsi vous finist ceste sarmoun,
Car du fraunceis i ad assez
E de meinte manere diversetez.
Dunc vous finist, seignurs, entaunt.
1140 Au Fiz Deu trestuz vous comaunt.
Amen.

Mace, cubebs and cloves and plenty of other spicery,   1124
Viaunde de Cypre and *maumenee*,[466] red and white wine in plenty;
Then plenty of other roasts, each alongside another,[467]
Pheasants, woodcocks and partridges, fieldfares, larks and plovers
    roasted,
Brawn, crisps and fritters or rose-sugar as corrective;   1132
And when the table was removed, blanch powder as whole
    sweetmeat
And other noble things in plenty. Now this lesson is over for you:
There's enough French here – and of all sorts of other things.
Gentlemen, it ends thus: I commend you all to the Son of God.   1140
Amen.

466. Surely not malmsey (as suggested in *AND* and by Rothwell 2009, p. 51
    note 11): there is no other evidence that this Greek wine was familiar in
    England so early. This is the dish *maumené*, as already seen by Hieatt and
    Butler 1985, p. 3. The manuscript reading is *maumerie* according to Rothwell,
    maumene according to Hieatt and Butler: palaeographically the difference is
    insignificant, but the latter reading also improves (though it does not perfect)
    the rhyme with *plenté*. A recipe is found in BL Royal 12.C.xii: *Maumenee: Vyn,*
    braoun de chapoun moudree tot a poudre e puis mis leynz pur boillyr ou le vyn;
    alemaunz moudrez tot seks e mys leynz; la poudre des clous mys ou tot frimailles
    d'alemaundes deivent estre mys leynz, e y doit estre char grosse moudree, sucre par
    abatre la force de l'especerie; colour, sorré ou ynde 'Maumenee. Wine; capon
    meat, ground thoroughly and boiled with the wine; dry-ground almonds
    added; add ground cloves together with fried almonds, and there should be
    beef, pork, or mutton, ground; sugar to balance the strength of the spices;
    the color, red or indigo' (text and translation from Hieatt and Jones 1986). For
    the same recipe in Middle English in *Diversa Cibaria* see Hieatt and Butler
    1985, p. 45. On the history of the dish and the name see Rodinson 1962. On
    maumenee recipes from England see Hieatt and Butler 1985, pp. 9–10.
467. An unsuccessful reworking of the line in the Trinity Feast: it is now unclear
    whether the dishes are beside each diner, or beside one another.